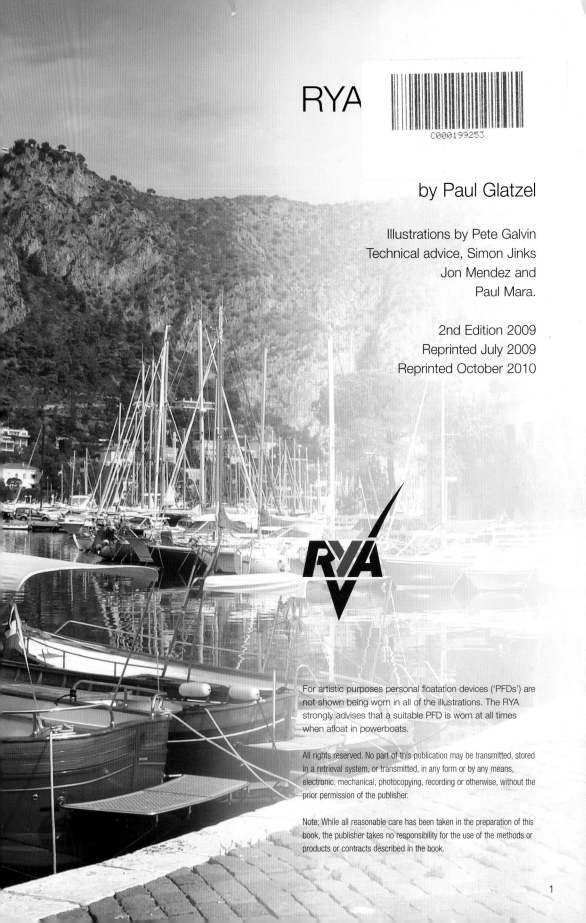

RYA

by Paul Glatzel

Illustrations by Pete Galvin
Technical advice, Simon Jinks
Jon Mendez and
Paul Mara.

2nd Edition 2009
Reprinted July 2009
Reprinted October 2010

For artistic purposes personal floatation devices ('PFDs') are
not shown being worn in all of the illustrations. The RYA
strongly advises that a suitable PFD is worn at all times
when afloat in powerboats.

Note: While all reasonable care has been taken in the preparation of this
book, the publisher takes no responsibility for the use of the methods or
products or contracts described in the book.

Foreword

The RYA Powerboat Handbook is designed to accompany RYA powerboat courses at RYA training centres around the world. It also provides a wealth of valuable information to all those thinking of going to sea.

More detailed information on specific subjects can be gained by reading:

RYA Day Skipper or Yachtmaster® Shorebased Notes.
These books cover the theoretical side of navigation, seamanship, meteorology and collision avoidance (Rules of the Road). They support the RYA Day Skipper and Yachtmaster® courses.

RYA An Introduction to Navigation (G77), RYA Introduction to Radar (G34), RYA Weather Handbook (G1), RYA Navigation Handbook (G7), RYA Boathandling for Sportsboats & RIBs (DVD 22).
These books give detailed information on specific subjects and are designed to be used by all boaters.

Practical courses

There is no substitute for experience. No matter how detailed the book, practical experience on board a boat with a trained instructor is worth its weight in gold. For the best possible preparation, use this book in conjunction with RYA tuition.

RYA practical courses include:

RYA Powerboat Level 1 Course
RYA Powerboat Level 2 Course
RYA Intermediate Powerboat Course (or RYA Powerboat Day Cruising Course)
RYA Advanced Powerboat Course
RYA Safety Boat Course

© 2009 Paul Glatzel 2nd Edition
First Published 2005
The Royal Yachting Association
RYA House, Ensign Way, Hamble
Southampton SO31 4YA
Tel: 0844 556 9555
Fax: 0844 556 9516
Email: publications@rya.org.uk
Web: www.rya.org.uk

British Cataloguing in Publication Date:
A Catalogue record of this book is available from the British Library.
ISBN: 978-1-906435-27-1
Acknowledgements: The United Kingdom Hydrographic Office, Piplers of Poole, Marinautic, Cobbs Quay Marina, The Met Office, Paul Mara, Clive Grant, Marlow Ropes, Reeds Almanac.
Photographic credits: Paul Glatzel, Chemring Marine, Premier Marinas, Seaward Boats, McMurdo, Piplers of Poole, Marinautic, Garmin, Icom, RNLI, Motor Boats Monthly, Scorpion RIBs, Tim Bartlett, Amberley Marine, Jon Mendez, PPL, Paul Mara, Laurence West, Simon Jinks, CHC, Raymarine.
Design: Creative Byte
Printed through: World Print
Cover Design: Pete Galvin
Proofreading and indexing: Alan Thatcher

Key to symbols

┄┄┄▶ Intended route

Engine ahead

Engine astern

Engine neutral

Stream

Wind direction

Wave direction

Boat direction

✓ Correct

✗ Incorrect

Contents

Introduction

Powerboating is an exhilarating, fun, and often, fast activity. In recent years the number of people involved in the sport has multiplied meaning that there are many more boats on the water. It has never been more important to acquire skills to make the sport safer and more enjoyable for all.

Whether you are a beginner or an experienced powerboater, this Handbook will help develop and expand your skills. It also acts as a useful resource for the RYA National Powerboat Scheme, and covers all of the areas of the syllabus; in fact, some subjects are covered to a greater depth than the level required.

All boats work along the principles set down in this book. Whether you are fishing or cruising the coast, the same pre-start checks will have to be done before leaving port, the same safety issues will need to be considered and the same manoeuvres have to be performed to get to the open sea.

Although it would be impossible to include every imaginable scenario in this book, we hope to give you the knowledge to assess a situation correctly and make an informed decision on what to do next.

Safety, preparation and briefing are the most important points to consider when going to sea. You must be well informed and prepared before you leave harbour. If in doubt during any manoeuvre or pilotage situation, slow down and give yourself time to think the situation through. Your aim is to think, at least one step ahead all the time, to try to anticipate what is going to happen next.

Becoming a capable and safe powerboater comes from a mixture of experience, training and common sense.

The RYA National Powerboat Scheme consists of a number of courses aimed at powerboaters with different levels of experience and different areas of interest. It is aimed at those using planing and displacement craft, both at sea and on inland waterways. The courses generally suit vessels up to about 10m, at which point the RYA Motor Cruising Scheme courses become relevant.

The RYA Motor Cruising Scheme courses are aimed at those using motor cruisers. These are typically planing or displacement craft, with accommodation, 10m and upwards in length either with single or twin-engined installations. The scheme consists of Helmsman, Day Skipper, Coastal Skipper and Yachtmaster® courses. These are available as both theory and practical courses. The theory courses are an excellent way to develop the theoretical knowledge before taking the practical courses.

Inevitably there is no clear divide between the Motor Cruising and Powerboat Schemes, and those seeking courses on craft around the *cut-off* point should chat to both a Motor Cruising school and a Powerboat school to find out which course suits their boating requirements.

RYA

getthe knowledge

RYA books for powerboating

RYA Boat Handling for Sportsboats and RIBs DVD

Jon Mendez

First of a new series of RYA DVDs focusing on key areas of boating skills. Essential to anyone new to powerboating, taking a RYA Powerboat Course or those wanting to perfect their skills.

DVD22

RYA Safety Boat Handbook

Essential reading for anyone involved in dinghy or windsurfer rescue at club level. Includes free DVD.

G16

RYA Introduction to Personal Watercraft

A 'must have' for beginners and those wanting to perfect their skills (formerly RYA Personal Watercraft Practical Course Notes).

G35

RYA Start Powerboating

Jon Mendez

The official course book for Levels 1 and 2 of the RYA National Powerboat Scheme (formerly Powerboat Practical Course Notes).

G48

RYA Introduction to Boat Handling for Sail & Power

Rob Gibson

All you need to know to become a competent and relaxed boat handler. Includes manoeuvring, marina work, rafting & anchoring.

G68

1 | Parts of a Boat

anchor locker

bow cleat

painter

compass

instruments

paddles

GPS aerial

VHF aerial

steaming light

A frame

radar reflector

flare box

outboard engine

bung

propeller

throttle controls

helm

kill cord

grab handles

navigation lights

lockers

transom

RIB (Rigid Inflatable Boat)

anchor

Ahead

Port Bow

foredeck hatch

pulpit

Port

GPS aerial

compass

VHF aerial

cockpit

Starboard Bow

sink

heads (toilet)

fridge

Port Quarter

instruments

Forward

navigation lights

outdrive

throttle controls

Starboard

Aft

cleats

Stern

Astern

fuel filler

propeller

fenders

Starboard Quarter

Sports Boat

2 | Types of Boats, Engines and Hulls

It is possible to have as much fun in a four metre boat as in a large twin-engine fast cruiser. Your choice of boat depends on its intended use and where it is to be used. Problems will arise if a boat is not used for its designed purpose, or used in areas where sea conditions are far worse than those intended for its design. When choosing a boat you should consider where you intend to use it, and what for.

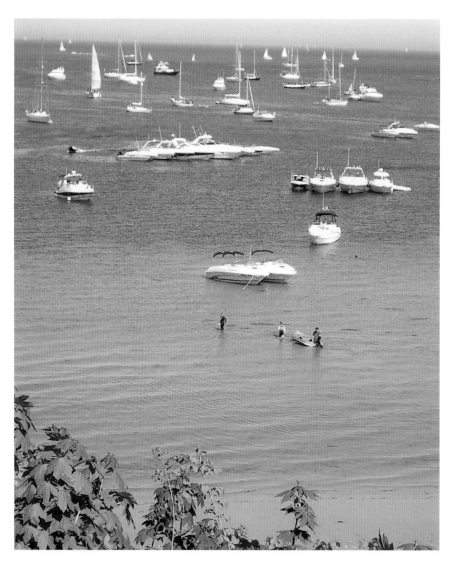

Choosing a boat

There are a number of factors to consider when choosing a boat:

- Intended use: A boat used for fishing in the winter is somewhat different to a boat used for water-skiing in the summer. Each boat is designed with a particular use in mind and it is important to choose one that will meet your needs.

- Boat budget: Boating is perceived as being expensive, but it need not be. A small second-hand powerboat can be bought for the same price as a PC system and can be an ideal starter boat. A large budget need not mean more enjoyment.

- Running costs: Buying the boat is only the first part of the cost. Fuel, equipment and storage should also be budgeted for. Fuel will usually cost more afloat and there can be a difference in costs between diesel and petrol. To store the boat in a marina, boat park or have the trailer serviced could cost a significant amount, while insurance and servicing plus the initial outlay on safety equipment can all bite a large chunk out of your bank balance. Do your sums and get quotes on running costs before buying.

- Area of use: The intended area of operation will be a major consideration. An area with a strong tidal race and often choppy conditions requires a boat with the hull characteristics, strength and power to deal with them. The same boat used on an inland lake may well be slow when compared with other boats on the lake. Equally, boating in an area where quayside petrol is unavailable may influence your decision to buy a diesel engined boat.

In some countries boats are categorised by the type of water they are to be used on:

Sheltered waters Boats that operate in daylight only, in estuaries, inshore or inland waters, close to a safe harbour of refuge where shelter may be found within approximately one hour if the weather should worsen. Boats in this category are likely to be around 6m or less in length.

Inshore Boats that cruise along the coast, within ten miles of land and approximately four hours of passage time from a safe harbour or refuge in which shelter may be found, by day or night.

Offshore Boats that cruise around the coast and to different countries, making offshore passages of between 50 and 500 miles. Boats in this category are likely to be over 8m.

Boats and hull shapes

Dory hulls offer a reduced wetted area than 'V' hulls and plane easily. However, they tend to 'slam' into waves and are only suitable for inshore use. They are mainly found on sheltered waters and are very stable. The hull has a deeper 'V' forward, that flattens out aft. This gives better action through waves and good planing features.

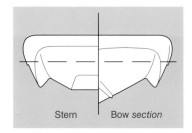

Stern | Bow *section*

Dory style vessels use a cathedral hull which gives a stable semi-flat bottomed boat with good speed in calm water. Good load bearing design but little grip in the water during turns. Excellent for lakes and sheltered waters.

Displacement hulls tend to be far more rounded and work by pushing water out of the way as they move. They tend to be slow, but very seaworthy. Their speed is governed by waterline length.

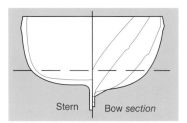

Stern | Bow *section*

Displacement boats are generally safe and slow boats with inboard engines. They may offer accommodation and some luxuries. Their speed is governed by the length of boat in the water but offer good sea-keeping qualities.

Catamarans have two hulls giving excellent stability and load carrying capabilities, requiring less power for the equivalent size vessel for similar performance.

Stern | Bow *section*

Catamarans are used as small ferries and fishing boats. They are also found on race boats as the reduced wetted surface area allows greater speed.

'V' shaped hulls are good in waves and rougher conditions. A deep 'V' hull slices through waves but tends to have less internal space because they have less beam (width). A flatter 'V' has a better beam but compromises its ability to slice through waves and may slam.

Stern | Bow *section*

Speedboat (4–8m) Small, fast, good for water-skiing and a family runabout. Hulls vary from very deep 'V' (generally boats with an offshore pedigree) to a flatter 'V', which potentially have better interior space due to a wider beam. Smaller boats mainly have outboards and most over 6m have inboard engines with an outdrive.

Fast fishers A popular style of boat due to its suitability for choppier coastal waters. They offer a sheltered wheelhouse and large open decked area at the rear. Although designed for coastal fishing they are also suitable as a family day boat. Some have fairly deep 'V' hulls that have the ability to cope with rougher conditions. Available with both outboard and inboard engines.

RIB - Rigid Inflatable Boat Designed initially for rescue and safety work, but increasingly popular as a family boat. Hull types range from deep 'V' to far flatter hulls. In competent hands, a well designed RIB can handle seas far in excess of those handled by other comparable sized boats due to their design and buoyant tubes. Lengths vary from 3m to 10m. Over 7m and inboard engines become available – almost exclusively diesel.

Fast Cruiser A great family boat offering a good mix of accommodation and deck area. Always inboard and mostly diesel fuelled. Upwards of 8m twin engine installations are quite common. The high topsides increase their windage, so care needs to be taken when berthing.

Stepped hulls

Developed originally for race boats, stepped hulls are now increasingly found on leisure craft and can give some performance advantages. (See Chapter 6 regarding handling a stepped hull boat).

Semi-displacement

Combines features of the 'V' shaped and displacement hulls. Good seakeeping, not overly quick though and need lots of power to go fast.

Stern | Bow section

Engines and drives

Outboards Outboard engines are by far the most common engine and drive system on small powerboats. The major advantage is that they are a self contained engine, drive and steering system that can be easily removed for service or replaced without much skilled work. Outboards are nearly exclusively petrol/gasoline powered.

Outdrives In effect, the lower part of the outboard is bolted onto the transom of the boat, but the engine is inside the boat. This is the most popular option for medium to large size powerboats as it allows for better weight distribution by placing the engine inboard. Also the engine gets better protection from the elements and is easier to service in the boat. The outdrive leg is steered left or right using a wheel.

Shaft drives Shaft drives are common on ski and working boats and increasingly on some of the small fast fishing type craft. A shaft drive allows the engine to be positioned further forward to aid the interior design or weight distribution. The propeller shaft attaches to the engine, runs through waterproof through-hull fittings to the propeller. A separate rudder is used to steer the boat using thrust from the propeller.

Jet drives The positioning of engine and drive unit is similar to that of an outdrive. But this time the engine drives an impeller, that sucks in water through a grille and jets it out under high pressure through a small hole to produce thrust. A steerable nozzle directs the jet of water to give power and steerage. A deflector ('bucket') is used to give ahead and astern control.

Forward facing drives These drive units are a recent development and whilst similar in some aspects to outdrives they are positioned below the hull with the props facing the front of the boat. They are typically the preserve of larger vessels above 11 – 12m and can be combined with a joystick for close quarter manoeuvring.

Twin-engined installations Boats often have twin outboards. Twin outdrive or shaft installations are usually the preserve of boats over 8m. Depending on the particular circumstances this offers more power and a safety net should one engine fail. A key feature of twin-engined installations is the ability of a craft to turn within its own length at slow speed by running each engine in opposite directions – one ahead and one astern. This turning effect is more limited where the separation of the engines is much less than 1m.

Pros and cons of types of outboard The choice of outboard engine is between 2-stroke and 4-stroke petrol/gasoline engines although emissions legalisation means that the vast majority of new engines sold are now 4 strokes.

Here are some comparisons:

4-Stroke	2-Stroke
• Very good fuel economy and very quiet running. • Oil is permanently in the engine crankcase like a car engine. • Sizes are available from a 2hp to 350hp.	• Lighter than comparable 4–strokes, so a better power to weight ratio. • Most 2-strokes are less fuel efficient than 4-strokes, newer models are getting better. • Oil is consumed and is either added to the fuel or kept in an oil reservoir.

Outboard engines (shows tiller control, only present on some smaller outboards)

1. Fuel tank
2. Fuel filler
3. Fuel tank vent
4. Fuel line
5. Fuel bulb
6. Oil filler - inside cowling
7. Starter battery
8. Battery isolator switch
9. Outboard leg
10. Cooling water tell-tale
11. Propeller
12. Cooling water inlet grille
13. Engine hand-start
14. Gear-operating lever
15. Transom mounting bracket
16. Throttle control
17. Kill cord

Throttle system

1. Single lever control
2. Fast idle control (some boats only)
3. Kill cord
4. Ignition switch
5. Gear lever interlock

Tip - always attach the Kill Cord to yourself when the engine is running.

Inboard engines

These tend to be available on craft 6m upwards and are usually found on sportsboats over 7m and all sports cruisers. Single engines are used up to 8m; above this twin installations are more popular. Either outdrives or shafts depending on the boat.

1.	Fuel tank	8.	Oil filler
2.	Fuel filler	9.	Cooling header tank
3.	Fuel tank vent	10.	Starter battery
4.	Fuel line	11.	Battery isolator switch
5.	Fuel filter	12.	Outboard/outdrive leg
6.	Oil filter	13.	Propeller
7.	Oil dipstick	14.	Cooling water inlet grille

Inboards vs. outboards

In most cases, the decision is determined by the boat you buy, although larger RIBs and some of the fast fishers often give you the option.

Inboards	**Outboards**
• Available in petrol or diesel.	• Far more reliable than in the past.
• Diesel may be the preferable option when waterside petrol is not easily available.	• Too complex for anything other than basic troubleshooting.
• Can be cheaper and simpler to service as they are essentially marinised car or truck engines.	• Can be raised out of the water at rest to prevent weed growth.
• Often provide a sundeck area above the engine.	• Far better power to weight ratio than comparable inboards.
	• Diesel outboards are available, although rare.
	• Possible to remove outboards for easier servicing.

Throttle systems

Many throttle controls for outboard and outdrive installations on boats up to about 8m have a small safety catch which needs to be engaged to allow the throttle to be used. Throttle systems are very basic. They allow forward drive, reverse drive or neutral to be engaged. Pushing the throttle 'forward' increases power to quicken the boat's speed through the water.

Starting procedure

The engine starting procedure varies from boat to boat, so this section acts only as a guide. Depending on how, and where, you launch and start your boat, many of these checks can be carried out beforehand.

Consult the owner's manual for starting instructions specific to your boat. Engines and throttle systems vary but the pre-start checks may include:

Pre-start checks	Starting
• Check fuel level and fuel turned on.	• On outboards - squeeze bulb to prime fuel.
• Turn batteries on.	• Attach kill cord to yourself.
• Check engine oil level.	• Ensure that engine is in neutral.
• Check drive leg and trim-tab oil levels.	• Engage choke.
• Check coolant level.	• Set throttle control to 'Fast Idle'.
• Check drive belts for condition and tension.	• Check prop is clear.
• Check raw water filter is clear of weed and obstructions.	• Start engine.
• Ensure air vent on tank is open.	• Check cooling water 'tell tale'.
• Vent engine bay using blower.	• Reduce throttle as engine warms.
	• Test kill cord works.
	• Engage gears briefly to check operation.

Bowthrusters

Bowthrusters are increasingly common on small boats now. The bowthruster is controlled from a joystick on the helm and pushes the bow of the boat either to port or starboard. They are used to neatly bring the bow alongside a pontoon or improve the angle of approach at slow speed. Only a small amount of power is needed, otherwise too much movement is created.

Fuel Choice

When choosing a boat with an inboard engine there may be a choice between petrol or diesel engines. Here are some comparisons between petrol and diesel engines.

Petrol	Diesel
• Petrol engines are less expensive to buy.	• Diesel inboards are more expensive than petrol engines to buy.
• The fire risk is higher.	• Fire risk is lower.
• Operating costs can be higher due to poorer economy although many direct injection engines are more economic.	• High usage will often make the extra initial investment of a diesel engine worthwhile.
• Sometimes refuelling via cans is the only and often impractical option.	• Diesel engines are generally more reliable and safer than petrol engines.
• Trailered boats can fill up at petrol stations instead of afloat.	• They are usually heavier than petrol and their power to weight ratio is less.
• Petrol engines require a qualified mechanic on all but the simplest problems.	• Many diesel engines operate using simple engineering that can be fixed at sea.
• They require electrics to run and the damp atmosphere onboard can hinder operation.	

3 | Propellers

The propeller transmits the power from the engine to create propulsion.

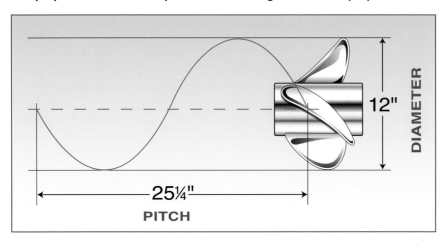

Pitch and diameter

Propellers ('props') are measured by their pitch and diameter.
- Diameter is the actual diameter of the propeller and blades and usually increases with engine size.

- Pitch is the theoretical distance the craft will travel on one rotation of the propeller. The actual distance travelled will be less due to slippage.

- Both pitch and diameter are generally measured in inches, however some metric dimensions are now being used.

Types of propeller

- Aluminium is the most common material for outdrive and outboard propellers. It is cost effective but can be easily damaged if it comes into contact with hard objects. However, the blades can usually be repaired fairly cheaply by a specialist.

- Stainless steel propellers are far stronger, can withstand more abuse, but are more expensive. The extra strength allows the blades to be thinner than their aluminium equivalents, which improves performance. However, should the propeller strike a hard object, the force can be transmitted through into the gearbox and may cause damage.

- Composite props are increasingly common, especially as spares. Some even allow blades to be replaced if one becomes chipped.

- Bronze props are commonly found on shaft drive craft such as ski-boats.

- Surface piercing props are the domain of race boats and high performance craft, and are designed for top-end speed. Optimum performance is acheived when only the lower half of the propeller is in the water.

How many blades?

• Three blades - Offer good top speed but less low down punch for acceleration.

• Four blades - Offer very good low-end acceleration, good for pulling skiers or working in rough conditions, but at the slight expense of top-end speed.

• Duoprops have two contra-rotating props on one shaft and usually two three-bladed propellers. This allows greater performance and the elimination of prop-walk. In effect the pitch is twice that of a normally propped boat, therefore it tries to drive forward twice as much for the same revs, doubling the efficiency.

Choosing a propeller

Finding the best propeller for your boat depends on your boating needs. Most people will be more than happy with the prop that is fitted to the boat as standard. Sometimes, because of how you use the boat, it may be worth changing the prop to increase efficiency. If you are constantly pulling skiers, choose a prop that gives you more torque at low power. If you were solely focused on speed, you should choose a prop that may be slow to get onto the plane but achieves a higher top speed. For some boaters, choosing and changing a propeller to optimise performance becomes a pastime in itself, but for most, the prop originally fitted by the engine manufacturer is satisfactory.

Propeller problems

Ventilation When exhaust gases or air from the surface are drawn onto the blades of a rotating propeller it may fail to grip and may rotate rapidly with a sudden increase in revs and loss of speed. This can give rise to cavitation.

Cavitation Occurs when the pressure at the blades of the propeller drops, allowing water on the blades to boil creating minute air bubbles. These bubbles contain considerable energy and, as they break down, can literally eat away at the blades' surface. Stainless steel props, being far stronger, can withstand this attack better, and are less susceptible as the blades are thinner.

4 | Safety and Planning

'Safety is a matter of common sense and state of mind', however once you decide to go afloat, there are a number of things to consider; the type of boat, how to handle it and how to plan and execute trips safely. As the skipper of a powerboat you are responsible for the safety of your crew, and boat. Having a great time on the water starts with good preparation and planning. This includes preparing the boat, ensuring the weather is suitable, briefing your crew and checking that you have the correct equipment for your intended passage.

We all have a responsibility to other water users to ensure we operate the boat sensibly and in harmony with others. Keep wash to a minimum around other craft, stay well clear of moored craft, sailboats and canoes and stay to the correct side in narrow channels.

Covering every aspect of your journey

Planning your day

Weather

Weather is discussed in more depth in Chapter 19. However, the key issue is should you go to sea in the first place? Use various sources of information to understand the conditions you will face. Take into account the experience of yourself, your crew and the capabilities of your boat. If you are in any doubt, do not go. Making this decision is not always easy, but as skipper you are responsible for everyone's safety.

Where to go

This is governed by many factors, but make sure you choose an area suitable for your boating needs and level of experience. If you are trailing a boat, check if a launch site a few miles further on may provide easier and safer launching and more sheltered sea conditions. Contact local marinas, chandlers and tourist centres for advice.

Many harbours and ports have their own local bylaws covering:

• Speed limits and quiet areas.

• Approved water-ski and jet-ski areas.

• Local collision regulations.

These can be obtained from harbour offices, almanacs and marinas.

Personal equipment

If in sunny climates ensure you take adequate protection from the sun, include long sleeved shirts and hats. Wet and cold climates are made worse by wind chill exacerbated by the speed of the boat. Consider taking waterproof clothing, gloves, dry suits and helmets. Children get cold very quickly, so plan your trips accordingly.

Other personal kit can include sun cream (high protection factor); medication (and instructions); water; snacks; waterproofs, warm clothing; personal buoyancy; suitable footwear; sunglasses; sun hat; towel.

Boat equipment

You do not need to spend a fortune equipping a boat. It is more important to have the correct safety gear than the latest electronic gizmo. Inexpensive purchases can be made via: boat jumbles, web based auction sites, mail order catalogues or simply by shopping around the multitude of chandlers' shops. The equipment carried depends on the intended area of use. It is vitally important that both you and the crew know how to operate the safety equipment. Ensure the equipment is stored in dry accessible places and consider marking lockers containing important items so that everything can be found easily.

Some items will depend on the area and particular use of the boat. Items to consider including the following.

Boat equipment: anchor with warp (rope) and chain, radar reflector, kill cord and a spare, tool kit and engine spares, compass, mobile phone, flares, fire extinguisher(s), a fire blanket, lifejackets or buoyancy aids, bilge pump or bailer, charts, watch or clock, first-aid kit, GPS, hull repair kit (e.g. wooden bungs) or tube repair kit, paddles or auxiliary outboard, mooring warps and fenders, throwing line, water, navigation-lights, horn, relevant shapes, VHF radio (fixed or hand-held), knife, almanac.

Extra equipment for longer offshore passages: EPIRB (a distress transmitter using satellites), PLB (Personal Locator Beacon – for man overboard situations), hand-held VHF, depth sounder, lifebuoys with lights, Chartplotter or simple GPS unit, hand bearing compass, binoculars, liferaft.

Kill cord

Most powerboats have an engine cut-out device called a kill cord. One end is attached near the throttle and other around the helmsman's leg. If the helmsman falls out of the boat, the engine cuts out. Runaway powerboats have caused serious injury and death. Test your kill cord to ensure it works. Spare kill cords should be carried so the boat can be re-started and driven back to the person in the water. Attach the cord around your leg or buoyancy aid/lifejacket and not to your wrist.

Lifejackets and buoyancy aids

A lifejacket is designed to turn an unconscious casualty in the water face up, keeping their head up out of the water. A buoyancy aid will keep a person afloat but will not turn them face up.

Lifejackets

Most adult lifejackets are gas inflation models, and are comfortable to wear and easy to store. Inflation is by a small gas canister and is activated manually or automatically when in contact with the water. Lifejackets are good all round performers and excellent for children and anyone less confident in water. Children should only use gas inflation lifejackets though if they can swim and are confident in the water. For younger or less confident youngsters permanent buoyancy lifejackets should be worn.

Auto and manual gas inflation: A person entering the water unconscious is unable to inflate a manual gas inflation lifejacket, therefore auto lifejackets are generally preferable. Take care to store automatic lifejackets in a dry area as some will inflate accidentally if the mechanism gets very damp.

Fitting crotch-straps to a lifejacket (if correctly worn) ensures when a person is in the water the lifejacket fits properly and doesn't ride up round their head.

Regularly check your lifejacket to ensure it will work when needed, checks include:

- Ensure it hasn't been activated - particularly if others may have used the lifejacket since you last did – are the 'green' indicators there?

- Is the gas cylinder tight in the mechanism, if possible remove it to ensure has not been used.

- Does the light work?

The manufacturer will supply you with detailed maintenance procedures; however other safety checks could include:

- Is there abrasion damage to the inflatable chamber?

- Check gas cylinder for signs of corrosion.

- Are the trigger mechanism and cylinder in date?

At least annually consider a full service by a chandler/the manufacturer.

Buoyancy aids

These provide buoyancy but will not turn an unconscious casualty upright, or provide as much support as a lifejacket. They are designed for watersports such as dinghy sailing, windsurfing and waterskiing. Often worn by powerboat drivers on safety boat duty overseeing a race or training, they are useful in smaller boats where having both lifejackets and buoyancy aids are impractical.

Skipper's responsibilities

Whether you are new to boating or a very qualified and experienced boater, as a Skipper you have a legal responsibility for the safety and well being of your crew and to other water users. You also need to ensure they enjoy themselves too!

As Skipper it is essential that you take responsibility for planning places to go that are realistic for the boat and crew. Good Skippers are calm, communicate clearly what they want, ensuring before any task is undertaken the crew know what is expected. Good Skippers do not panic if things don't go as planned and err on the side of caution always realising that their crew's safety is their primary concern. They are considerate to their crew and other water users and appreciate they are constantly learning every time they go afloat.

Before departure, ensure that you are aware of any non swimmers (insist they wear their lifejacket) and understand medical conditions that your crew may have, know where their medication is kept and how it is administered (Attending a basic first aid course is a sensible precaution for a Skipper).

Skipper's safety briefing

Once ready to go afloat, give your crew a safety briefing covering the following:

- Use of lifejackets.
- Location and use of flares.
- Use of VHF - how to send a Mayday message.
- Location of first aid kit.
- Location and use of fire extinguishers.
- Engine starting procedures and kill-cord use.
- What the plan for the day is including rough timings.
- Basic boat handling - so that they can get back to you if you go overboard.
- Deployment of liferaft (if fitted).
- Anchoring.
- To ask if any thing you ask is unclear.

Deck brief

Before departure go through the basics of tying up. Take the time to practise tying up and coming alongside. Explain well in advance what you are doing.

Good communication with your crew will keep them informed and involved and will help them enjoy the experience more, this will only be achieved if they know what they are supposed to do.

Once out at sea, do remember that even though you may love going fast, your crew may not be so confident, and they could become frightened. You know what you are going to do – your crew don't, so throttle back and introduce them slowly to your sport.

Tip - Make sure you know your responsibilities under SOLAS V - see Chapter 23.

Summoning assistance

If a problem arises, you should know what action to take and how to deal with it. Your first consideration is: are you, the crew or boat in immediate danger? If yes, call for assistance immediately.

The most common methods for raising the alarm where there is grave and imminent danger are:

• A VHF radio Mayday call.

• Flares.

• Arm signals, sound horn, mobile phone.

If the problem is less serious, as an example your engine has stopped working, you may well flag down another boat, call the Coastguard or a boatyard on either VHF or a mobile phone to arrange for a tow.

VHF radio

How you raise the alarm using VHF depends on whether your radio is equipped with Digital Selective Calling (DSC). This allows some messages including a Mayday to initially automatically broadcast digitally rather than by voice. A DSC radio should receive position information from a GPS (Global Positioning System). At the touch of a button, the nature of the alert, the craft's identity and position is sent out in a fraction of a second.

DSC equipped VHF radio

There are two steps to making the call:

• Sending the digital distress message

• Making a follow up voice distress call

Sending the digital distress message

• Remove the cover on the red 'Distress' button and press the red button for 8-10 seconds (Some sets need you to press the red button momentarily before you do this).

• A digital alert is broadcast to all DSC equipped craft including the local Coastguard Station.

• The alert will include your MMSI - if you have programmed it into the radio - your position and the time. The MMSI is a unique number identifying your craft.

Making a follow up voice distress call

Mayday, Mayday, Mayday
This is powerboat Fleetwood, Fleetwood, Fleetwood,
MMSI 234001234
Mayday Fleetwood,
My position is 50° 30'.5N, 001° 57'.5W, approximately 5 miles south of Anvil Point, Have hit submerged object and am sinking.
Four persons on board
Immediate assistance required
Abandoning to the liferaft
Over.

- You should immediately receive a digital reply from the Coastguard, followed by a voice reply on Channel 16.

- No other stations should use Channel 16 while the Coastguard is 'casualty working'.

Non DSC equipped VHF radio

Follow the procedure outlined above for the voice distress call via Channel 16 but without the digital element of the process.

Pan-Pan calls

If your predicament is less serious than a Mayday situation then the Coastguard will still assist you if you call with "DSC Urgency Alert" followed by a Pan Pan call on channel 16. A 'Pan Pan' call indicates you require assistance but there is no immediate danger to life. It is also used if a person on board requires medical attention or advice.

It is an offence to use a VHF radio without a licence – except in an emergency. Contact your national boating authority for details of VHF courses.

Mobile phone

A mobile phone can in some situations be useful. In an emergency, calling the emergency services and asking for the Coastguard will connect you to the local Coastguard Operations Room. Programme the phone numbers of local organisations and friends who could offer assistance. Remember, mobile phones are not usually waterproof and reception depends on cell coverage which can be patchy at sea. A SMS text message will have a better chance of getting through.

Tip - When stating your position, quote the position as a 'lat and long' taken from your chart or GPS, e.g., 50° 30'.5N, 001° 57'.5W, also explain it in simple terms as "approximately 5 miles south of Anvil Point". More craft will then know where you are and be able to offer assistance.

Flares

Flares are an essential item of safety equipment but there are many different types and makes and a variety of ways they operate. Familiarise yourself with their operation. It is good practice to carry only one make of flare on board to prevent confusion when you need to use them.

Recommended number to carry	Inshore	Sheltered waters
	Within 10 miles of shore day or night	Small craft in harbours, estuaries, close inshore and inland. Daylight only
Red parachute flare The most effective long range flare; projects a bright flare to about 300m. Do not use near helicopters!	2	0
Red hand-held flare Indicates precise position of craft, use when close to other craft or land.	4	2
Orange hand-held smoke Use in daylight, useful for attracting helicopter or lifeboat attention.	2	2
White hand-held Collision-avoidance flare; use to alert other craft to your presence.	4	0

Tip - Flares have an expiry date 3-4 years from manufacture. Ensure your flares are in date.

Stow flares in a waterproof box. Place foam at the bottom and around the sides to soften impact on the flares. A pair of gardening gloves will help protect hands when handling them.

Attend a flare demonstration or course where you can let off real flares.

Launch and Recovery

Unless the boat is kept in a marina berth, launching and recovery by trailer will be a key aspect of where to go afloat. The decision on which slipway to use depends on the type of boat, the needs and interests of your crew and security for the vehicle and trailer while you are afloat.

Launching

Go to any public slipway and you will see plenty of examples of safe and easy launches alongside some dangerous and stressful ones: the difference being good planning and preparation.

Planning

- Where will you launch? Some slipways are public and free, many are privately owned and a fee must be paid.

- Check if there are local bylaws to consider, some areas allow only certain types or sizes of boats.

- In some areas a permit is required to use a boat.

- Some slipways are suitable only for smaller craft, while others have a walkway or dock alongside, making launching easier. Others end abruptly leaving the trailer wheels stuck in the mud at low water.

- Ensure your tow vehicle will cope. Rear wheel drive vehicles will struggle on a slippery slope, while front wheel drives suffer from wheel spin if the weight of the trailer is excessive. Choose the slipway and launch method which suits your vehicle.

- Check the local tide tables in advance to ensure you have enough water for launching and recovery.

- Are conditions safe for launching? Strong winds, especially if they are blowing onshore, can make a launch very difficult and dangerous.

Preparation

- On arrival, park well away from the slip.

- Remove the tailboard, straps and boat cover.

- Insert the bung and check the hull for damage in transit.

- Load the boat with equipment and supplies.

After a long journey let the wheel bearings cool for 45 minutes before launching. Immersing hot wheel bearings earlier may create a vacuum as the bearings rapidly cool, this draws in water and washes out the grease from the bearings.

Launching

How far the trailer is reversed into the water depends on the gradient of the slipway, the size and weight of boat, and how easy it is to launch from the trailer. The rear of the boat needs to float so that it can be reversed or pushed off the trailer. Car wheels are best kept well away from sea water.

- Manoeuvre the trailer to the top of the slipway. Keep vehicle windows open to aid communication and in case vehicle rolls into water.

- Reverse down the slipway if possible only partially submerging the trailer's wheels (to preserve the bearings and brakes) then push the boat off the trailer or hop into the boat and reverse it away.

If the gradient of the slipway is shallow which prevents you launching with the trailer attached to the car, use a rope or metal extension bar to enable the trailer to be reversed further into the water.

- At the top of the slipway, chock the wheels, put the handbrake on, lower the jockey wheel and then disconnect the trailer.

- Connect a long line between the trailer and the tow hook using bow lines.

- Drive the car forwards to take up the slack in the line. Remove the handbrake and slowly reverse down the slipway while an assistant keeps the trailer in line.

- An assistant may need to enter the water to ease the boat off.

Tip - Launching with a rope between the vehicle and trailer can be useful to keep the tow vehicle's wheels clear of the lower slippery part of the slipway and water.

Danger - To avoid the boat sliding off the trailer when backing down the slipway: ensure the winch strap remains attached to the boat along with an additional safety chain or line between the boat and trailer.

Recovery

In many instances it is possible to stop the boat whilst drifting towards the slip, jump out when the water is shallow enough and hold the boat until the trailer comes into the water. On other occasions, especially where the slip is steep, it is best to drive the boat onto the trailer.

Driving onto a trailer

This technique requires careful throttle control and more care is required than with a manual recovery. The helmsman needs to line up the approach to the trailer compensating for wind and stream, arriving at the trailer so that the forward 'V' of the hull aligns centrally on the trailer.

- Ease the trailer into the water so that it is partially submerged and allows the boat to drive on to it.

- Trim the engine up so that the prop does not ground on approach, ensure that cooling water is still circulating.

- Drive the boat on to the trailer compensating for wind and stream.

- For safety reasons you should get out of the boat when it is towed out of the water.

- When the boat is on the trailer, either attach the winch strap to the forward D-ring or lash a line from the boat to the trailer.

- If a rope or bar was used, chock the wheels and reattach the vehicle to the trailer.

- Ideally, flush the engine cooling system (see page 34) with fresh water and give the boat and trailer a hose down.

If your engine does not have a dedicated flushing point, use a hose attached to muffs to direct fresh water to the intake. Start the engine and run in neutral for three to four minutes. Check your engine manual for 'care after use' details.

Danger - If launching or recovering with the trailer detached from the tow vehicle, ensure the trailer is well in the water before pushing the boat off or winching it on. The nose of the trailer can be forced rapidly skywards as the weight transfers to the rear of the trailer.

Serious injury can occur when boats roll off trailers with the winch strap attached and the winch handle rotating rapidly. Use the safety lock to prevent this happening. Never grab a winch handle if it is spinning.

Before towing

- Ensure the boat is fully secure on the trailer.

- Use tie-down straps on the D-rings on the transom to hold the rear of the boat to the trailer.

- Connect the D-ring on the bow to hold the front of the boat in position.

- Use a safety chain between the vehicle and the trailer as the two may become detached - except for braked trailers.

Tip - Steep slipways and heavy boats can cause serious harm; so take things slowly. Plan what you are going to do and double check everything before you start. Remember a good launch is one that is slow, controlled and safe.

Boat Handling |

Being able to helm a powerboat safely and with confidence starts with an understanding of the way a boat handles and how the elements of wind and stream affect its behaviour. Experience and practice will build your level of confidence. This section will show you how to get the most from your boat in a variety of situations.

The basics

A powerboat is moved forwards or backwards by the rotation of the propeller which pushes or pulls the boat through the water. Increase the throttle and the boat will move more as the prop turns faster. Engaging forward gear creates forward effort by thrust coming from the prop or drive-unit. Engaging neutral stops the thrust, however you may still be moving forwards due to momentum. Engaging reverse (astern) rotates the propeller in the opposite direction to stop the boat or move it astern. The steering wheel diverts the water flow from the propeller to turn the boat by turning the outboard, outdrive or rudder. Several other factors need to be considered before you start.

Pivot points

In forward gear, boats pivot at a position approximately just forward of the centre of the boat. In reverse the pivot point is near the stern of the boat, the engine in effect 'pulls' the craft around. You are turning the back of the boat and it takes a while for the front to react. These differences in handling can be used to good effect by a skipper when handling at slow speed around a marina or near pontoons.

 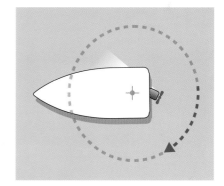

Propwalk

Propellers push the boat forward, but because of their rotation they also make the stern move to one side. This effect is called propwalk (or paddle wheel effect) because of the tendency of the prop to "walk" the stern to one side. It is most evident when going astern. All boats have propwalk, and prop and hull design dictate its effect on the handling characteristics of the boat. However, propwalk on outboards and outdrives is negligible.

Going astern, a right-handed prop will walk to the left (port). Some boats will walk around in a large circle whilst going astern, while others have negligible prop walk and reverse in a straight line. In use, the forward prop effect will be hardly noticed – the overriding effect on the boat will be the 'kick-to-port' in astern, and most close-quarter manoeuvres will be affected by this, especially on single shaft vessels.

Tip - Check for propwalk whilst tied alongside. Ensure the rudder is straight, engage astern gear and observe which side the wash comes out from under the hull. Wash to starboard suggests a kick to port in astern. It is useful to establish which way a single prop boat kicks before manoeuvring out of the berth.

Streams

Streams are caused by either tide, natural river flow or by local movement of water, as occurs around locks. Streams have a similar effect to stepping onto a conveyor belt, moving you bodily in one direction.

If you motor in the same direction as the stream, the boat travels quicker past the shore and reaches its destination faster. If motoring against the stream it will take longer to reach your destination. Even though you may be travelling through the water at the same speed, your speed over ground will be less.

When coming alongside, a boat pointing into the stream is slower over the ground retaining good steerageway, allowing better control.

Stream can also push you into or away from danger. To assess the stream's direction, look for its signs:

- Bubbles in the water flowing past a moored boat.

- Moored boat leaving a wake.

- Tight mooring lines indicating pressure from one side.

- Weed on the pontoon floats flowing down-stream.

- Water stacking up around piles and buoys.

If you are still unsure of stream direction, motor slowly across the water and look ahead at two points in line (a transit) to check for drift. It is worth noting that the stream can be stronger further from the shore, and that there is sometimes a reduction in its rate in a marina or dock. When both wind and stream are opposing each other, assess which is the stronger by motoring slowly across the stream and gauging which way the boat is being pushed.

Wind

The forces of wind and stream have an effect on how the boat manoeuvres. Because planing boats have very little grip on the water, the wind can blow them across the water's surface. Displacement boats are often heavier so may initially be less affected by the wind.

Be aware of wind direction. You can assess the wind direction by looking at:

- Flags around the dock.

- Wind indicators at the top of yacht masts.

- Wind ruffling the surface of the water.

- By fitting a flag or wind indicator to your boat.

The effect wind has on a boat is twofold.

- Firstly, if the boat is moving slowly or has stopped, wind drifts the whole boat sideways. Sideways drift can be used to advantage in some coming alongside techniques. Good spacial awareness is required to avoid drifting downwind and onto obstructions.

- Secondly, because the bow has less grip in the water than the stern (where the props and rudders are), the wind will always blow the bow away first. Therefore it is quite difficult to keep a motor cruiser bow into the wind. Left to lie naturally, it will sit beam to wind or with the wind on one quarter.

- The easiest way to hold position in wind is to reverse gently and sit stern to wind. Reversing moves the pivot point aft. The stern will seek the wind and the bow can be allowed to blow downwind.

Tip - Use stream and wind to advantage to aid manoeuvring. Find out which has the greatest effect and use it as a brake.

Turning principles

Single shaft A single shaft drive boat is turned using bursts of ahead and astern. These bursts are applied only when the wheel is turned hard over.

Outboards Steer the boat when the propeller is moving. If the engine is in neutral then the steerage effect is reduced as the outboard has a decreasing effect as a rudder, as the vessel slows.

Outdrives These have similar characteristics to an outboard but the engine is inside the craft.

Twin outdrives The outside engine has greater leverage. This can be used to good effect in a turn. To turn hard to port, turn the wheel to the left, engage forward on the outside (starboard) engine, and a sharper turn will be achieved.

Twin shaft As with twin outdrives the outer engine has greater leverage. The engines can be used alone to effect a turn, one driving ahead and the other astern.

Twin engines or shafts make a craft far easier to control, however, on smaller craft, where the engines are less than 1m apart, the effect of twin engines is lessened. Where they are placed further apart they have more leverage, and both engines can be manipulated to steer the craft.

Turning single shaft

A single shaft drive boat is turned using bursts of ahead and astern applied when the wheel is turned hard over, so that the rudder deflects the burst of prop-wash straight away and its power is transmitted into the turn and not into forward progress. Typically a burst is 2 seconds, depending on conditions.

- Position the boat in the centre of the space. Start too close to one side and the stern may be in danger of clipping the pontoon.

- Approach slowly, speed carried into a turn makes the turning circle larger.

- Turn in the direction that the astern prop walk will aid the turn.

- Wheel hard over and give a burst ahead. Engage neutral.

- When the rate of turn slows or space ahead is limited, go astern. Changes in rudder position are ineffective as there is insufficient space to gain steerageway. Momentum and prop walk are now turning the boat.

- Once the correct direction is achieved, straighten the wheel. Select ahead.

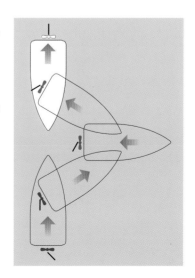

Turning a single outdrive or outboard

Turning with outdrives requires constant use of the wheel, because the wheel controls the direction of the prop wash. To achieve the tightest turn, the wheel should be turned before the prop is engaged so that valuable turning space is not used up driving the boat forward. Wash from the prop driving astern is directional and is also used to help the turn.

The order:
Neutral – turn wheel – ahead – neutral – reverse wheel – astern. Repeat the sequence until the turn is completed.

In all cases, the pivot point on outdrive boats is further back when going astern. This has the effect of making the bow drift very quickly in wind when reversing. If the bow does start drifting uncontrollably, let it and the stern will seek the wind. Reverse into the wind to make more space and then recover the manoeuvre by motoring forward.

1 Motor slowly into the space.
   Stop.
   Wheel hard over to starboard.
   Engage ahead.
   Monitor the turn.
   Neutral when space is short.

2 Wheel hard over to port.
   Engage astern.
   Monitor turn.
   Neutral when space is short.

3 Straighten using wheel.
   Engage ahead.

You don't need to achieve the turn in three stages – take as many as are necessary.

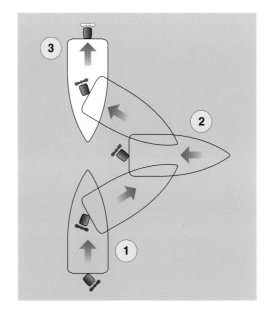

Tip - The golden rule when boat handling in close quarters is to turn the wheel first, then apply the gear. This immediately diverts the prop wash or thrust in the correct direction.

Tip - If it all goes wrong, put the engine into neutral and fend off. Do not power out of the problem. Think it through and remember to have an escape route planned.

Turning a twin outdrive or outboard

- Use opposite wheel lock to engine, wheel to right (starboard), use left (port) engine.

- Remember pivot points move further aft in astern.

- Change wheel position between motoring ahead and astern.

1 Motor slowly into the space.
Stop.
Wheel hard over to starboard.
Ahead port engine.
Monitor the turn.
Neutral when space is short.

2 Wheel hard over to port.
Astern starboard engine.
Monitor turn.
Neutral when space is short.

3 Wheel hard over to starboard.
Ahead port engine.
Monitor turn.
Straighten helm when turn is completed.

Turning a twin shaft drive boat

Twin shaft drive ('screw') boats are very manoeuvrable because each propeller is positioned to make the most of the pivot point. A tight turn is achieved using both throttles simultaneously. Using port engine ahead and starboard engine astern twists the boat around in her own length. Using both engines combined with the wheel to starboard creates the smallest turn as the rudder diverts the prop wash from the port engine. It may be easier to start by using one engine at a time, then move on to simultaneous use.

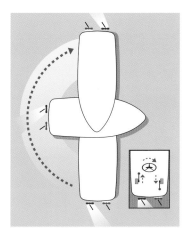

Tip - All boats handle differently, try using the methods for twin screw boats on your twin outdrive or outboard craft to see how it handles. You will soon start to use elements of both techniques as confidence grows.

Tip - On twin engined boats resist the urge to push throttles further apart to deal with an issue. For example, when turning using each engine against each other, to reduce forward momentum go to neutral on the engine in forward gear rather than increasing revs on astern engine.

Handling a jet drive boat

Jet drive boats are increasing popular on leisure craft and are used widely in the commercial world. At slow speed the techniques needed to manoeuvre the vessel are different to both shaftdrives and outboard/outdrive arrangements. Instead of using forward and reverse the drive is left permanently in forward and the boat is propelled through the water by a jet of water directed backwards in much the same way as a propeller does, e.g. steer to the left and the boat turns to the left. To go astern though another lever is used to position a 'deflector' (referred to as a 'bucket') in the path of this jet of water. The shape of the deflector and the direction the water is deflected typically means that if your helm is to the left (to port) then the rear of the craft goes to the right (starboard). The deflector can be positioned at any point between fully ahead and fully astern making a jet driven boat highly manoeuvrable.

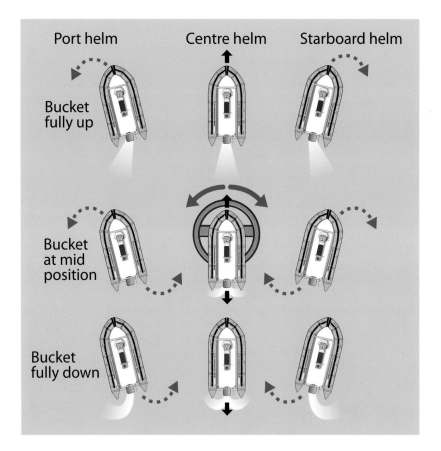

Slide

Controlling a boat is a little like controlling a car on an icy road, they both slide or drift. Turn to starboard and the boat will slide out of the turn to port because it has little grip on the water's surface. A turn at greater speed increases the slide. Try not to start a turn too late as the slide may well take you towards other vessels.

Turning through 180°

When turning a boat it is usual to turn towards the wind especially in a confined space. Once the bow is through the wind, the wind will help push the bow in the desired direction. It is very important to keep an eye on the wind and stream direction and watch out for slide and drift on your approach.

- Wheel hard over.
- Engage Ahead.

  When the bow is into or through the wind:
- Engage neutral and reverse the wheel.
- Go astern.

  Just before the boat is pointing in the correct direction:
- Engage neutral.
- Reverse the wheel and go ahead.

Pivot point moves aft

Remember

- The wind may help the turn but may blow you towards other craft, so leave enough space.
- Wheel first - then power.
- Pivot point moves aft in astern.
- Outdrive boats are very light at the bow and you will lose the bow very quickly in a strong breeze.
- A bow thruster can make the turn easier but many are not powerful enough to push the bow through the wind.

Tip - If the elements take over; the bow will disappear downwind quite rapidly. Let it, and then reverse away as the stern will seek the wind.

7 | Leaving and Coming Alongside

Leaving a pontoon or berth

Coming away from a pontoon is a relatively simple manoeuvre. If the route ahead is clear and there is no wind or stream, then for small boats a good push off the pontoon and driving away forward can do the trick. However, larger craft require you to drive it off.

Coming away in reverse is often the best way to leave a berth.

- Steer away from the pontoon.
- Engage reverse.
- As the stern comes away straighten up the wheel.
- Once well clear move off ahead.

As boats are more curved at the bow than the stern it is sometimes possible to fender the bow area well and motor gently towards the pontoon for a second to push the stern away from the pontoon. This creates space for the stern to reverse clear. This is especially true for single shaft drive craft.

Twin outdrives

Here is a case for not using opposite helm and engine. Turn the helm to the left and put the left engine in astern. This tends to lift the boat from the dock.

Twin shafts

Protect the bow with fenders and go astern on the inside prop. If there is an onshore wind you might need to turn the helm towards the dock and use a touch of ahead from the outside prop or use a bow line to pull against.

Using a line to assist leaving a berth

If the wind is pushing the boat onto the pontoon, or if the berth is restricted, motoring against a line can allow the stern to get into clear water and allow an easy exit.

Reversing on a bow line

- Rig up a bow slip line.

- Fender the bow well.

- Steer away from the dock.

- Engage astern.

- The stern starts to pivot away from the pontoon into clear water.

- Engage neutral.

- Slip the bow line and reverse away.

Danger - Never hold on to the line. Always secure the line to a cleat.

This works well for all craft with the exception of single shaft drive. On twin engine vessels use the engine nearest the pontoon.

Bow spring line

- Rig a bow spring line and fender the bow area.

- Motor forwards to bring the bow in and the stern away from the pontoon.

- Engage Neutral.

- Slip the spring and reverse away.

This works well for single shaft drive craft.

Danger - Moving away forward on any vessel can kick the stern into the pontoon.

Coming alongside

Tight manoeuvring among pontoons and other boats can be made far easier and less stressful with planning and preparation, and by taking into account how the wind and stream will affect the boat. Before approaching:

- Consider what the wind and stream are doing. How will they affect your approach? Approaching into the wind or stream will act as a brake to the boat. Ideally, approach into whichever will have the greatest effect.

- Brief your crew so they know exactly what is expected of them.

- Prepare fenders and lines.

- Plan your 'escape' route, in case the plan goes wrong.

The idea is to berth the boat in one flowing movement and with practice this can be achieved.

The process can also be broken down into smaller steps to make it easier to understand.

1 Start your approach as far off the pontoon as is practical. Your angle of approach should be about 30°–40°. Keep speed to a minimum by using neutral.

2 When close, steer away from the pontoon and engage forward gear momentarily to bring the boat alongside. Ideally, you should glide to a stop alongside the pontoon. Be prepared to go astern to stop.

3 You can also slow the boat and bring the stern in by turning the wheel towards the dock and applying astern momentarily.

Tip - Remember when coming alongside a berth your objective is to do so safely, accept that you might not always do it perfectly though - no-one does! Never let your crew jump onto pontoons from the boat - teach them to lasso cleats from the safety of the boat (see Chapter 15).

Wind off pontoon

Just as we have used lines to help us leave a berth, we can also use them to help us get alongside. These techniques are especially useful if the wind is blowing the boat away from the pontoon.

1 Attach a bow line to a cleat on the pontoon (lassoing the cleat is the easiest method – see page 71).

2 Turn the steering wheel towards the pontoon. Engage reverse at tick-over/idle.

3 Craft moves slowly alongside. Attach stern line and take out of gear.

In certain circumstances and particluarly in craft that are affected significantly by the wind or have poor bow access it can be easier to let the stern seek the wind and reverse towards the pontoon.

1 Fender the stern well and watch out for bathing platforms (if fitted). Watch for lines in the water.

2 From within the safety of the cockpit area; the crew lasso the stern cleat with the stern line, leaving 1-2m of line between the stern and the pontoon.

3 Steer towards the pontoon and engage forward at tick-over speed. The boat is then 'driven' alongside the pontoon.

Twin engine

Using one engine at a time, motor slowly towards the pontoon. When the cleat is near the bow, stop the boat, lasso the cleat with the bow line, take up any slack and secure. Engage tick-over astern on the outside engine. This pulls back on the bow line and pivots the stern towards the pontoon. When the stern is close to the pontoon, secure.

Mooring in a marina

Coming into a marina berth requires extra care because there are moored boats and vessels moving around.

If you are visiting, call the marina office on your VHF to establish which side to put your fenders out. 'Starboard-side-to' means your lines and fenders will be placed on the right if you enter the berth facing forwards.

Assess the effects of wind and stream on the berth you are going to, if necessary go and look at the berth before deciding on exactly how you are going to approach it. Brief your crew on what you want them to do, ensure lines and fenders are ready and the crew will not leap onto pontoons. Plan an approach that allows minimum speed into the berth and if necessary plan to go past a berth, turn and approach it from a more favourable direction to make the approach easier.

With limited wind or stream you will aim to come in as slowly as possible, when there is lots of wind or stream though, you may need to be prepared to use lines or to come into the berth slightly faster to overcome the effects of wind or stream on the boat. You can decide all of this in your initial assessment.

Consider these marina berths:

A Approaching into the wind will naturally slow the boat but on boats with lots of windage be careful not to lose control of the bow. The momentum of the boat will help it slide sideways alongside the berth.

B The turning momentum will tend to slide the boat away from the berth. Consider going beyond the berth, turning and approaching from other direction.

C As the stern seeks the wind in astern, this boat reverses easily into the berth.

D The wind will push the craft into the berth, so care is needed not to overshoot. Put a stern line on early.

E Reversing in stern first with the bow into the wind may be very tricky as the wind will try to push the bow so the vessel is lying beam on to the wind. A bowthruster would make things easier if fitted.

> **Tip** - Rather than one sweeping movement into the berth stop short, position the boat then drive in using the minimum amount of speed necessary.

> **Tip** - On many boats rigging a line to the mid-ships cleat so that either the crew or helmsman can slip it over a cleat when entering a berth can make it easier to bring the boat alongside the berth.

Using a bowthruster

Do not hesitate to use a bowthruster if you need it. Ensure it is switched on and works before you approach a berth. Use small amounts of thrust to compensate for the effect of wind on the bow of the craft. Practise your handling to ensure you are not overly reliant on it though.

Mooring in wind and stream - Ferry gliding

It is possible to drift a boat sideways by steering into the elements using gentle throttle turning the boat slightly so that the wind or stream is pushing on one side of the bow, thus enabling you to 'crab' sideways in that direction. This is called ferry gliding and it can be used to come alongside pontoons or other boats in a slow, controlled manner.

Stern-to and bows-to mooring

Mooring in many locations is often stern to or bows to the quay. Powerboats usually moor stern to the quay for ease of access to the shore. Stern lines are used to stay close to the quay, while the anchor or a line attached to weights or chains on the seabed holds the boat away. A passerelle or wooden plank, carried by the boat, is used to go ashore.

Holding off using an anchor - The approach

- Rig up fenders on both sides and a large fender on the stern. Rig stern lines from both quarters.

- Prepare to drop the anchor.

- Reverse towards the wind.

- Four boat lengths away from the quay drop the anchor and ease out chain.

- One boat length from the quay, stop easing the chain so that the anchor digs in. Be ready to let out more chain if required.

- Connect the windward stern line to the shore, followed by the leeward stern line.

- Once positioned the correct distance from the quay, take the strain up on the chain.

Holding off using pre-installed chains or weights

Lazy lines are used in tight harbours and marinas where it is unsuitable to drop the anchor because it may become fouled. Instead of an anchor holding the bow away, the bow is connected to a heavy bow line, which is attached to a concrete block or chains. The bow line is also attached to a lighter line, which is led to the quayside for ease of retrieval.

The approach

- Rig up fenders either side and at the stern.
- Rig two stern lines.
- Reverse towards the quay.
- Connect windward stern line to quay.
- Pick up lazy line, lead to bow and tie off.
- Connect second stern line.
- Adjust bow and stern lines.

It is possible to hold the boat in position once the windward stern line is attached by applying small nudges ahead on the leeward engine.

Tip - If it is safe to do so, have a crew member forward with a roving fender ready to fend off from craft adjacent to you.

In very windy conditions or a difficult berth consider dropping a crew member off to tend lines for you, or if short handed call the marina for assistance.

Mooring buoys

Mooring buoys are laid by individuals and harbour authorities for permanent moorings and visitors. Most visitors' buoys have markings and in some areas their position is noted on a chart or pilot book.

Buoys vary; some have obvious rings on top and others have chain loops hanging from below attached via a line to the pick up buoy. Never tie off to the pick up buoy.

Before picking up a mooring buoy consider:

- Choose a buoy that looks strong enough for your boat, ensure it isn't just attached to a lobster pot!
- Check there is sufficient depth now and for the duration of your stay.
- Ensure it will give shelter from the present and forecast wind.
- Assess direction of stream and wind to decide best direction of approach.

- Pick up buoys float downstream and are a good indication of stream direction.
- Sailing boats and powerboats often sit in different directions with wind and stream. Sailing yachts have a keel and this is affected more by stream than wind. Powerboats have little grip on the water and tend to lay with the wind.

- Initially stop your craft to assess the effect of wind and stream on it. Ideally you want to approach the buoy using wind and stream to slow your approach. To determine what direction to choose look at other similar style boats on moorings, they will usually be pointing in the direction you should use. Alternatively having stopped your craft let it drift and then, if possible, approach from the opposite direction to the direction of drift.
- Alternate between neutral and tick-over forward so your approach is slow and controlled.
- Judge your speed by looking sideways at passing objects.
- You require the minimum of speed while still having full control.
- If you do overshoot, go into neutral to avoid tangling the mooring in the prop.
- If mooring to a buoy with a ring use at least two turns around the ring as the movement will chafe through the line.
- If using a pick-up buoy ensure that you connect to the heavy line attached to it and not the light line on the buoy itself.

- With some craft, where it is difficult to pick up a mooring buoy from the foredeck, consider approaching astern.

- Rig a line from a forward cleat back to the cockpit area.

- Reverse up to the buoy.

- Tie off as described above.

- The vessel will then swing round.

- For a short stay in light wind, rigging a single line from a stern cleat to the buoy or from both stern cleats in a V shape works well.

> **Tip** - If you are moored to someone else's mooring buoy, a crew member must stay with the boat and be prepared to move it should the owners return.

Locks

In tidal waters locks are found at the entrance to marinas, harbour basins and rivers that would otherwise dry out at low water. These locks are usually controlled by a lockmaster and entry is often controlled by a traffic light system.

On inland waterways a series of locks are often found allowing a vessel to climb or descend an incline. At the entrance to marinas or harbours they are usually single locks with many vessels seeking to enter or leave.

Consult an almanac for instructions or call the lockmaster by VHF or mobile phone for permission to enter. Assess the effect of wind or stream across the entrance of the lock and rig fenders both sides as a precaution. Some locks have pontoons to tie on to that rise or fall with the water level, whilst others require you to slip lines around a riser bar or bollard.

Anchoring 8

Anchoring allows you to stop for lunch or overnight in quiet and pleasant surroundings away from the crowds. It is also the first line of action if the engine fails in shallow water because it stops the boat and allows the problem to be resolved.

There are various types of anchors. The choice depends on your chosen cruising ground. Some anchors have good holding in mud and sand, others are designed to pierce weed and get in between rocks.

A strong anchor with good holding power.

A flat anchor with good holding, always lies flat.

A good anchor with excellent holding.

Almost a fixed version of the Plough (without the hinge) often used by craft with electric anchor winches, as it resets itself well into the bow roller.

All of these anchors have good holding in a variety of surfaces. The one best suited to your needs is dependent on your boat type, the area you will be anchoring in, and how easy each will be to stow. Other anchors include:

Poor holding versus recommended anchors.

Awkward to stow and heavier than other anchors of similar holding power.

Not often used by small sports boats but useful for river craft.

Things to consider before anchoring include:

- Look for a sheltered anchorage.

- Take a trial run to assess depth, and allow for a falling tide.

- Avoid main channels and submarine power lines; use charts to identify areas.

- Prepare the anchor line and anchor.

- How much rope and chain needs to be put out?

- Check charts for obstructions and what ground to expect.

DEPTH   SCOPE

ALL CHAIN = 4 x DEPTH   MIXED CHAIN & LINE = 6 x DEPTH

The anchor is connected to a 'scope' of chain, or a chain and rope combination. The amount of scope let out when anchoring depends on whether the scope is all chain or a mixture. The more scope you let out reduces the chances of the boat snatching the anchor out of the seabed. It also acts as a shock absorber. If in a tidal area you need to allow for the rise of tide in your calculations.

The amount of scope carried on board depends on your area of operation. In shallow estuaries 30m would be sufficient whereas in deep and rocky areas considerably more may be required.

Dropping the anchor

The process of anchoring is very similar to picking up a mooring buoy. RIBs and speedboats with open bows are easier to anchor, because going forward is easy. On larger craft with anchor lockers at the bow, a crew member must go onto the foredeck to anchor but with caution, keeping their centre of gravity low.

- Look for shelter.

- Check depth.

- Approach chosen anchor point in same direction as you would for a mooring buoy.

- When at the chosen point stop the boat.

- Drop the anchor to the seabed.

- As vessel drifts back, ease out scope to 4:1 (all chain) or 6:1 (rope/chain) ratio.

- Make fast and engage reverse briefly to dig the anchor in.

Dragging and swinging

Yachts and powerboats move in different ways as the stream or wind changes.

Check your anchor is not dragging by:

- Identifying a transit and checking it at regular intervals.
- Setting up the anchor-drag function on your GPS.
- Taking a bearing from a hand bearing compass.

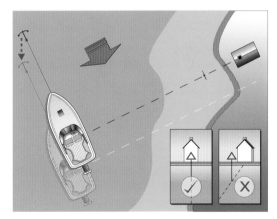

- If the objects in transit cease to be lined up or the bearing changes, you are dragging.
- If your anchor is dragging, you will need to raise it and re-anchor.
- If it continues to drag choose a different anchorage.

Raising the anchor

- Check to see how the boat is lying.
- If the boat is pulling back away from the anchor, you may need to slowly motor towards the anchor as the crew pulls in the slack and raises the anchor.
- Good crew communication is essential to avoid overrunning and fouling the prop.
- Hand signals between crew and helmsman are useful.
- Bring the anchor and line on-board, and stow it away so it is ready for immediate redeployment.

Tip - Anchors stored in the bow lockers may do considerable damage if not secured.

Make sure your anchor line is suitable. Nylon is good, it is elastic and it does not float.

9 | Travelling at Speed

If your vessel is fitted with a kill cord it is essential to wear it at all times. At speed ensure that your crew have a good seating position, a firm grip, and know what you are going to do before you do it. They can only know what you are going to do if you tell them beforehand.

Avoid situations which involve rapid changes in direction. Take early action in potential collision situations and remember, if in doubt, take the power off reducing the closing speeds of vessels. Keep a good look out for other craft, keep a watch for and predict the effect of waves or the wash from other vessels. By keeping alert and assessing situations early, you can make high speed driving safe and fun.

Travelling at planing speeds

It takes a lot of power to get on the plane. Once there it may be necessary to throttle back slightly to ease speed and conserve fuel. A displacement or semi-displacement hull will never achieve the ability to plane on the top of the water so its speed will be governed by hull form and the power available.

Before accelerating ensure that the engine is either fully 'trimmed in' or to the neutral position depending on the craft. This helps the boat get up on to the "plane".

As the throttle is pushed forward a powerboat begins to move from being a displacement boat at low speed and starts to climb on top of her bow wave and get on the plane.

As speed increases, less of the boat is touching the water. This reduces friction allowing speed to to be maintained with less power.

Executing manoeuvres at planing speeds

Whenever turning at speed it is important to warn the crew so that they are not thrown out of the boat. Turning too sharply allows the prop to suck in air (ventilate) and lose grip on the water. Slowing the rate of turn or the amount of revs will allow the prop to grip again. Trim down before commencing a turn for greater grip and control during the turn.

Turns through 180°

When approaching a turn; set up the boat by trimming-in the leg, take off some speed, look around especially behind, warn your crew, then execute a wide turn keeping the boat on the plane by managing the throttle. If you turn too tightly most of the speed will be lost. Coming out of the turn apply power and trim-out.

S-turns

S-turns (gradual turns to the right or left) can be made at reasonably high speed as long as they are steady and controlled, when the conditions are suitable. Again use all round vision and communicate your intentions to your crew.

Stepped hulls

In turns some stepped hull designs can behave less predictably than 'standard' hulls and care should be taken to not trim in too far and to not reduce power suddenly in the turn. Consult the Owner's Manual and dealer for detailed instructions relating to your type of craft.

Balance - "trimming your boat"

You can trim your boat in two ways; fore and aft – raising and lowering the bow, and from side to side levelling the boat if it is leaning to one side.

Don't forget too that where you position people and kit in the boat will affect the trim of the boat too.

Leg in to start to keep the prop in the water and help the boat get on the plane.

On the plane ease the leg out to achieve the best speed. Ease out too much and the prop sucks in air from the surface, making it spin faster but lose grip on the water, therefore slowing the boat. Ease the leg out by the correct amount and the revs increase slightly without the throttle being adjusted, therefore speed increases.

If the boat starts to porpoise (the bow bounces up and down), trim the leg in to regain control, then slowly ease out to re-trim.

Trim may need constant adjustment. If crew move around the boat or there is a change in sea conditions or speed, you need to check the trim. Fuel use makes the boat lighter – you may need to trim differently when tanks are full or half empty.

Tip - Even when trim gauges are fitted, they can be unreliable. Practise in various conditions to get the best trim. When there are no gauges, use time increments to know whether the leg is up, down or centred. While in port count how long the tabs take to rise, lower and centre. When trimmed correctly the revs rise slightly and the helm feels lighter without pull to either side.

Trim tabs

Trim tabs are either flat plates or vertical blades fitted either side of the boat and attached to the transom. They are used to trim or level the boat, both fore and aft and side to side.

Trim tabs are controlled up and downwards by either a hydraulic, or electric ram system on the transom.

- Tabs down – raises the stern which in turn depresses the bow (bow down).

- Tabs up – lowers the stern which in turn raises the bow (bow up).

- As a basic rule you tab down into a head-sea and tab up with a following sea.

- Tabs can also be used to compensate for a beam sea or uneven loading.

- One tab down – raises one side of the boat. This is useful to compensate for loading irregularities or a beam sea.

Gauges are rarely fitted to advise you how much trim is used. While in port count how long the tabs take to rise, lower and centre, then use time increments for their positioning.

Tabs can be helpful when getting up on the plane. Tab down to lift the stern. Tabs should not be needed, but may help compensate for the crew standing at the rear or weed on the hull.

Although tabs are mainly used at speed, they can also be used tabbed down in marinas to increase grip on the water. Beware of powerful reversing when tabbed down, as this can cause damage to the tabs.

Tabs can make a huge difference to comfort and sea-keeping ability at speed. It is possible to achieve basic steering using one tab at a time.

Experimentation in different conditions will give the best compromise of comfort, fuel consumption and ride, but tab half down is a good starting point.

Tip - If you have trim tabs and the ability to trim the drive leg then try to keep it simple. Use power trim for fore and aft trim and trim tabs for side to side trim.

10 Difficult Conditions

At some stage everyone faces conditions at sea which test both their boat and self. Knowing what to do in these situations makes all the difference.

In rough conditions, try to match your speed and direction to the conditions by careful control of the throttles and steering. Jumping from wave to wave or ploughing through waves can be great fun, but yourself, crew and boat will find it very wearing. Make sure that everyone has good handholds and seating positions and the helmsman is wearing the killcord.

Driving upwind

Waves are generally generated by wind and come from the same direction. Driving into the wind therefore means driving into the waves. Driving downwind the boat drives with the waves, applying special techniques will ensure safety and comfort.

Driving upwind usually entails trimming down and driving up the face of the wave.

Ease off at the top of the wave to ensure you do not take off.

Accelerate down the back of the wave, speeding up to raise the bow as the trough is reached, then drive up the wave towards the next crest.

The ride then becomes smooth and quite fast. Progression is achieved by throttling on and off as you move over the wave. Trimming down ensures that the 'V' of the hull is used to slice into the approaching wave, while applying more throttle lifts the bow in the trough to drive up the approaching wave and prevent the bow driving straight into it. This avoids the need for trimming up and down to achieve the same effect.

Tip - Upwind - This can be summed up as: when the bow is rising - throttle back, when the bow is falling - throttle up.

Whether this proves to be a comfortable ride depends to a large extent on the 'wavelength' (the distance between the wave crests). Shorter wavelengths can make it very difficult, as there is little time between wave crests for the helmsman to adjust the throttle settings. In this case, you might find it easier to drive at 30°–45° to the wave front. This increases the 'apparent wavelength' and can therefore allow you to increase your speed and smooth your journey. You will then need to zigzag towards your destination but, while longer in distance, this method can be less stressful and quicker.

Beam seas

Large breaking waves taken on the beam have the potential to capsize a boat. Usually keep a fair speed, constantly watch for breaking waves, then steer a path behind, or in front of and away from them, as conditions dictate. The speed and power of your boat is key. If you get caught on the downwind side of a breaking wave, turn into the wave and power on to climb up the wave or turn away from the wave and try to outrun it.

Driving downwind

One of the most dangerous conditions for a sportsboat is a 'following sea' (the craft is running in the direction of the wind). If a breaking wave catches the vessel, the confused water catches the prop, reducing its ability to bite. The following wave then turns the craft side on to the waves making a capsize almost inevitable with the next wave. To avoid this, match the boat's speed to that of the waves. Another problem of going down the face of a wave is going too fast through the wave causing the bow to fall into the trough. The boat loses speed, the wave pivots the boat beam on and the next wave either swamps or capsizes the boat.

1 To make progress in these conditions, trim the bow up and ride the wave, staying behind the crest.

2 As it breaks, care is needed not to power through the breaking wave too early. As the wave breaks, you may need to ease the power in the confused water to avoid the prop losing grip and speed. A good look out must be kept behind at all times to avoid the chasing waves catching you up. Alternatively, pick a calm patch to turn into the sea and look for another port.

3 Watch the boat speed as you may need to ease the throttle, then power through to sit on the back of the next wave.

The conditions you experience may be magnified or reduced by the combination of wind, stream and the local environment. Wind in the opposite direction to the stream ('wind against tide (or stream)') can create short, sharp and unpleasant seas when driving upwind, yet markedly different conditions if driving downwind. Short, sharp seas can be difficult to deal with, as the helmsman has little time between each wave to recover and plan how to deal with the next one.

Harbour bar

When a large following sea is found at the entrance to a harbour, the conditions can get even livelier and generally should not be attempted. As the depth of water near land reduces the waves grow in height, break earlier and more violently and the change in conditions can be dramatic.

Water freeing arrangements

Open vessels such as dories and RIBs are susceptible to taking on board large amounts of water in rough conditions. If you have a craft like these then ensure that the arrangements to remove this water from the craft rapidly are adequate. As crew move to one side of a vessel then water in the vessel will move to that side potentially leading to a rapid loss of stability and perhaps the capsize of the vessel.

Search Patterns | 11

As you become more experienced, you may venture further off the beaten track and sometimes be caught out in less than perfect sea conditions. This increases the chance of you becoming involved in incidents requiring conducting a search or taking part in a helicopter transfer. Prior knowledge of what you and your crew should do will be a great advantage.

Search patterns

A search pattern could be used to find a crew member who has fallen overboard or to look for a person or boat that has been reported in the area. If you need to undertake a search, there are a number of considerations:

- Ensure the rescue authorities are aware of the situation. They will task SAR (Search and Rescue) resources to assist.

- If you have lost someone overboard, you should start your search in the area in which they are now most likely to be. They may have drifted some distance. The starting point is known as the 'datum' point.

It is important that the search efficiently covers the search area. It should also be simple enough for the crew to execute effectively. The simplest effective search is the 'expanding box search'.

Expanding Box Search

- 'D' is the 'Detection range' and is the maximum distance at which an observer in the boat can see a casualty in the water for half the time. A weighted fender or similar object may be used to calculate this range.

- The length of the leg grows every two legs.

- The direction of the initial leg is in the direction the casualty is most likely to have drifted, (although many people start 'north up' as it keeps it simple) and each turn is 90° to starboard.

Learning how to execute a search pattern should never be left until you have to do it. Find a suitable area of water, drop an item into the water and practise retrieving it with your regular crew.

12 | Man Overboard

A person falling overboard (MOB) is a serious situation, therefore:

If someone goes overboard

- Alert the crew by shouting 'Man overboard'.
- Instruct one person to point at the MOB at all times.
- If travelling at slow speed, turn the wheel back towards the MOB. This moves the prop away from the MOB.
- Effect a slow controlled turn back towards the MOB.
- Make a DSC distress alert and Mayday call.

Recovery

Return to and recovery of the MOB is the most important element. Make sure you know which recovery method best suits your boat and crew. Muscles lose their strength very quickly in cold water so do not expect much help from the MOB. Practise just in case you have to do it for real one day. Below are two recovery techniques:

Method 1 – Into the wind

- Give plenty of room and approach from downwind.
- Reduce power, then move slowly towards the MOB.
- Use neutral to control your speed.
- Keep the MOB on the windward bow.
- When close enough, remove all power and grab hold of the MOB.
- Switch off the engine*.
- Assist the MOB to an area of the boat where they can be recovered.

Advantages	Disadvantages
• Suits smaller craft with low freeboards.	• Need to be prompt at collection time.
• Allows waves to be taken head-on.	• Can lose sight of MOB under the bow.
• Good when rough as MOB is unlikely to go under the boat.	• Can be difficult if alone in boat.

*As skipper you need to balance switching off the engine for the safety of the MOB against the experience of the helm and the sea conditions you are facing.

Method 2 – Beam on approach

- Drive upwind of the MOB.

- Stop and position upwind of MOB.

- Slowly adjust position to drift down onto the MOB.

- When alongside switch off engine*.

Advantages

- Suits high-bowed vessels where sight of the MOB is easily lost while approaching them into the wind.

- Greater collection area - whole side of the vessel.

- Provides some shelter to MOB. Allows boat to be easily brought alongside MOB by cockpit area, where freeboard is lowest.

The Williamson turn

If it is night or poor light you may need to use the Williamson turn to return to the MOB. This requires a compass orientated turn to return back to the MOB. First alter your heading either way by 60° then reverse the turn onto the reciprocal of your original heading. The MOB should be in front of you as you are travelling the reciprocal of your original heading.

Disadvantages

- Can be uncomfortable beam onto sea.

- Small craft can be blown over the MOB.

Causes and prevention

- At slow speed, sharp throttle movements can catch people unawares. Brief crew before speeding up and ensure they hold on.

- Don't let your crew leap off the boat onto the pontoon, teach them how to use the lasso technique.

- At higher speed, ensure crew are seated and holding on. Beware of sudden wheel movements.

- Young children need full time supervision.

- Cover this in your safety briefing.

13 | Helicopter Rescue

If you or your crew require emergency evacuation a helicopter may be sent to your assistance. It is most likely that a helicopter crew will seek to undertake a 'high-line' transfer but helicopter procedures do differ from country to country.

- Before the helicopter arrives, prepare your boat for its arrival and secure all loose items.

- The helicopter pilot will make contact by VHF and give a brief on what is going to happen. Small craft are usually attended with the boat stationary, however the brief may give a course and speed you should follow. Listen very carefully and take notes.

- If asked to steer a course and speed it is important to keep to it without deviating.

- A weighted line is lowered. Let it earth in the water to release any static. Do not attach it to the boat. Pull on the line to guide the helicopter winch-man to the boat. Gloves are useful.

- Coil the line; a bucket is useful.

- The winch-man will land on deck, unhook and assess the situation. He now has complete authority.

- If the casualty needs to be removed from the boat the winch-man will take the casualty off the boat. You will use the weighted line to control his swing. Do not let it snag on anything.

Towing on the Water |

Good seamanship dictates that you should come to the aid of a boater in distress or needing assistance. Often this amounts to the request for a tow from a stricken powerboat or yacht.

There are two ways of towing:

Long tow The towed craft is attached on a long line to your own. This is suitable in areas of open water away from other craft.

Alongside tow When you are close to other craft (perhaps entering a marina), or a confined river where greater control of the towed craft is required.

Long tow

- Use the longest line practical as it acts as a shock absorber between tug and tow and reduces the strain on fittings.

- Form a short bridle around your transom. Doing this utilises the strongest points, spreads the load and centres the pull.

- The disabled vessel should either tie the tug's line to their D-ring on the bow, if fitted, or onto a bridle led from their two forward cleats.

- The length of the line should allow the vessels to be twice the distance between wave crests or troughs, this ensures that both boats ride the waves together, and reduces snatching.

- Snatching can be reduced by hanging a weight, such as an anchor, from the centre of the towline.

- The helm of the towed craft can steer to help the tug.

- If the towed craft is veering around as it is being towed, ask the skipper to move the weight aft or drag warps etc to give the stern drag and stability.

- Stay clear of main shipping lanes and channels.

- Inform the Coastguard.

The speed of the tow will be determined by the sea state and the power of the towing craft. Maintaining a low speed of 5–8 knots is best and reduces strain on both craft.

Side tow

The key to a successful side tow is correctly setting up the position of the craft relative to each other and ensuring that suitable lines are rigged between them.

Key points are:

- Fender the boats well.

- The rudder or engine of the towing vessel should be set well behind the stern of the towed craft.

- The towed craft should be angled slightly into the towing vessel.

- The spring line between the bow of the towing vessel and the stern of the disabled craft takes about 100% of the strain when towing forward. The spring from the rear of the towing vessel to the bow of the disabled craft does so when towing in reverse.

- Towing vessel 'angled in'.

- Towing vessel well astern.

- Spring 'f' takes load in forward. Spring 'r' in astern.

Being towed

If you need a tow, ensure:

- The tow craft is capable of the tow - a 4m speedboat might be keen to practise towing on your 8m cruiser, but is it safe?

- Salvage: Agree a price at the outset for fuel or a few beers once at the slipway. It's also good practice to offer them a line you have prepared as evidence that you retain control of your vessel.

Manoeuvring

The two tied vessels have distinct handling characteristics. Once you understand these, precise towing is quite straightforward. Think of the set-up as a twin-engined craft with only one engine working. The outside engine on the turn has the greatest leverage.

Turns easily = small turning circle.   Difficult to turn = large turning circle.

Tip - Before commencing a tow you should consider whether you and your boat are capable of the tow. Your first responsibility has to be to your own crew. Taking on a tow beyond your and your boat's capability would be foolhardy. Call for professional assistance if necessary.

15 | Knots and Rope Work

You do not need to know how to tie a large number of knots, but make sure you can tie a few knots well.

Bowline

This is probably the most useful knot to be able to tie, and has a variety of uses:

- The loop can easily be draped over a bollard, tow ball or cleat.
- Two bowlines can be easily tied together joining two lines.

It can take a very high load, but cannot be untied under load.

Round turn and two half-hitches

This is useful for tasks such as tying to a mooring buoy or ring. It is also very useful for tying fenders on to rails, and tying covers down tightly.

One of the key benefits of the knot is that once the turn is on, the knot can be tied and untied while under load.

Clove hitch

Generally used for tying fenders on. Also used to tie on to bollards.

This knot should only be used under low loads as it can jam and be hard to undo.

Sheet bend

This is useful for joining two ropes together as, for example, to extend a mooring line.

Threading the smaller rope (in the image) through a second or third time creates a safe knot less likely to come undone.

Taking a turn and tying to a cleat

Because large loads come onto a warp, keep fingers a safe distance away from the cleat.

Take a full turn around the cleat – this takes the load of the boat whilst still allowing the warp to be eased or taken in.

A figure of eight takes more strain, then two more turns complete the sequence – the boat is now secure and the cleat may be left.

Coiling and stowing a line

Open your left palm and lay equal sized coils into it. As each coil is laid, turn the line between your thumb and forefinger clockwise. This has the effect of creating neat coils. Finish off by wrapping the line around the coil. Thread the end through the coil to secure.

Throwing a rope

Coil the line as described above. Separate the single coil into two smaller coils. Ensure that the end of the line is secured, and then throw the coil. Allow the other coil to play out from an open palm.

Lassoing a cleat

Secure one end of the line to the cleat onboard and secure the other end by standing on it. Coil the line, then separate the coils into two smaller coils. Holding one coil in each hand, when close enough to the cleat you intend lassoing, throw both coils to land either side of the cleat.

Types of rope	
	3-strand polyester Many versions of polyester come 'pre-stretched'. These are not very good for anchoring or mooring. Polyester is harder wearing.
	3-strand nylon Has excellent stretch properties, is good for mooring, anchor lines and towing. Easy to splice. Suffers some loss of strength when wet.
	Dockline A nylon line with a harder wearing polyester cover that is generally used for mooring. Available in a variety of colours.
	Anchorplait High elasticity and ease of coiling into an anchor locker make this an excellent choice for anchor lines. Is also used for mooring lines.

What lines should you carry?

Smaller powerboats tend to carry two main lines which are used for mooring. These should be approximately twice the length of the boat and each can be used to tie off at the bow and stern. They should be long enough to be run back to the centre of the boat as spring lines (red). 'Springs' are tied to prevent the craft moving backwards and forwards on its berth. It is good practice to carry two spare lines, both of which are twice the length of the boat.

The anchor line should be as long as possible and can double as a tow line if not spliced to the chain. Estimate the depth in places where you go boating, multiply the depth by six and buy a line of that length. In practice, a small powerboat may have an anchor line long enough for a typical anchorage plus an extra 30m line stored away in case the need arises to tow, or for emergencies.

Collision Regulations

How craft avoid each other at sea is covered by the International Regulations Preventing Collisions at Sea (IRPCS).

A skipper has a legal responsibility to follow these rules. Most are common sense, for example:

- You have a responsibility to follow the rules.

- You must keep a good lookout.

- You must avoid a collision by taking clear and obvious actions.

- Always use a safe speed.

Because powerboats are very manoeuvrable, they usually give way to all other types of craft (e.g. sailing boats, rowing boats, fishing vessels, vessels restricted in their ability to manoeuvre or not under command).

The first question is "Does a risk of collision exist?" If there is a risk, then both skippers have responsibilities. One is deemed the 'stand on' vessel and the other the 'give way' vessel. If both obey the rules this works well - however, there is no absolute right and wrong and you <u>both</u> have a duty to avoid a close quarters situation or a collision.

Common Sense

A 4m powerboat and a supertanker at sea are governed by these rules. However discretion is the better part of valour. Common sense dictates that it is far better to keep well clear of a potential collision situation than test the larger craft's readiness to give way. The supertanker might be: Constrained by its draught in a narrow channel and unable to turn, or a vessel may be restricted in its ability to manoeuvre, towing, trawling or dredging.

A – The RIB is crossing the channel at right angles to cross it as quickly as possible.

B – The large craft is constrained by its draught and will keep to the centre of the channel.

C – Smaller craft can keep outside the channel if there is enough depth, but still pass port to port.

How can you predict if a risk of collision exists?

If relative bearings between two vessels remain constant, a collision will occur unless action is taken to avoid it.

Irrespective of whether you are the 'give way' or 'stand on' vessel, you have a responsibility to avoid each other and must take every precaution to avoid a collision.

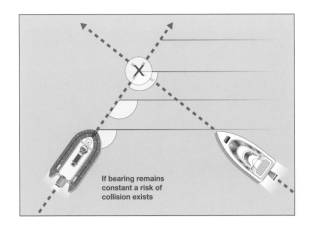

If bearing remains constant a risk of collision exists

Danger - The stand-on vessel should avoid a turn to port.

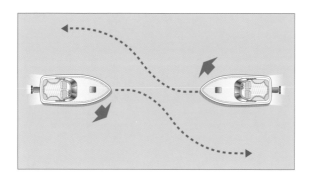

Head on

Each vessel must make a clear and obvious turn to starboard in order to pass port to port well clear of each other. If no risk of collision exists, craft can pass well clear of each other, starboard to starboard.

Crossing situation

The stand on vessel should hold its course and speed (but continue to carefully monitor what action the other vessel is taking), while the give-way vessel should alter its course and/or speed to stay clear of the other vessel.

Give way or stand-on?

- You are the give way vessel in a crossing situation if you see the other craft approaching from the starboard (right) side. If it is approaching from port (the left) then you are the 'stand on' vessel.

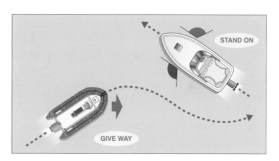

- At night you would see red (give way) or green (stand on) aspect lights.

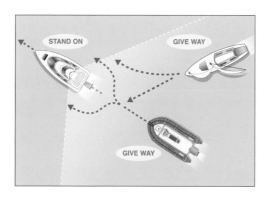

Overtaking

An overtaking vessel (one which falls within an arc of 135° at the rear of the craft being overtaken) must keep well clear of the vessel it is overtaking. The vessel being overtaken must maintain its course and speed.

Giving way to vessels under sail

- Powerboats unless being overtaken must give way to vessels under sail.

- Keep well clear of sailing vessels as they may make large adjustments to their course as they 'tack' or 'gybe'. Remember, your wash can seriously disturb smaller craft.

- A yacht sailing with the assistance of its engine is 'motor sailing' and should display a cone with the point facing downwards in the rigging. The yacht is then classed as a motorised vessel under the rules.

Knowing under what circumstances sailing vessels give way to each other can help you decide what action to take when you are approaching them.

Sailing vessels cannot sail directly into wind and therefore use a zig zag course (tack) upwind.

Whether a sailing vessel is the give way vessel or the stand on vessel, is determined by which 'tack' it is on. The tack a yacht is on is indicated by looking at its sails, and by which side of the yacht the wind is blowing into. If the wind is blowing into the sails over the port side of the craft then it is on 'port tack'. If the wind is blowing over the starboard side into the sails it is 'starboard tack'.

Yachts on different tacks Yacht on Port tack gives way to yacht on Starboard tack.

Yachts on same tack Yacht nearest the wind ('to windward') gives way.

Restricted visibility

When visibility is restricted, proceed at a safe, slow speed and use all available means to keep a lookout. Vessels fitted with radar should make best use of it. If possible head for shallower water away from larger vessels.

Lights, shapes and sounds

At night vessels display navigation lights to indicate the type of vessel and the position of the lights helps indicate the vessel's direction. By day, shapes are hoisted to indicate the nature of the vessel.

Fog signals

—— One long blast (4-6 seconds)   o One short blast (1 second)

	At night	By day
A vessel under 7m and 7 knots. A single white light could also be a vessel at anchor or a vessel seen from astern.		
A powered vessel under 50m shows port and starboard lights and either a white masthead light and a white stern – light or, if under 12m, a single all-round white light. Fog —— every two minutes.		
A powered craft over 50m displays two masthead white lights – the forward one lower than the one at the stern – a white sternlight and its port and starboard lights. Fog —— every two minutes.		
A yacht under sail either shows a tricolour; or port and starboard lights plus a white sternlight. If the engine is used, it becomes a power vessel and must display the appropriate lights. Its day shape when motor sailing is a cone pointing downward. Fog —— o o every two minutes.		
At anchor under 50m only one white light is required. The day shape is a black ball. A vessel over 50m at anchor displays two white lights, with the stern one lower than the bow one. In fog at anchor: <100m Rapid ringing of bell for 5 seconds every minute >100m Bell rung forward, gong aft for 5 seconds every minute.		
Code flag A indicates a vessel engaged in diving operations – keep well clear. At night 'Restricted in ability to manoeuvre' lights are shown.		

	At night	By day
A vessel 'not under command', (perhaps a vessel adrift with no means of propulsion) displays two all-round red lights at night or two balls in daylight. Fog — ○ ○ every two minutes.		
If constrained by draught the vessel displays 3 all round vertical red lights or a cylinder during the day. Fog — ○ ○ every two minutes.		
Vessel 'Restricted in ability to manoeuvre' shows an additional all round red-white-red combination of lights at night and ball diamond ball in daylight. Fog — ○ ○ every two minutes.		
Vessel engaged in fishing (but not trawling), displays an additional all-round red light above its all round white. Two cones apex together by day. Fog — ○ ○ every two minutes.		
A vessel trawling displays an additional all-round green light above its all round white. Two cones apex together by day. Fog — ○ ○ every two minutes.		
A vessel involved in dredging shows restricted in its ability to manoeuvre, plus two all-round vertical reds to show which side its gear is out and two all-round vertical greens showing the side that is safe to pass. In daylight, diamonds indicate the safe side and balls indicate the side not to pass.		
A vessel towing displays an additional white masthead light if the tow is less than 200m, or two additional white masthead lights, if it is greater than 200m. By day diamonds are shown. Fog — ○ ○ every two minutes. For both types.	OVER 200m UNDER 200m	OVER 200m UNDER 200m

	At night	By day
A flashing orange light is seen on vessels that travel in non displacement mode - examples include: hovercraft or very fast passenger ferries.		
A Pilot vessel displays an all-round white over red plus its aspect lights and displays a red and white flag in daylight.		
A Minesweeper shows three all-round green lights in a triangular pattern at night or three balls in daylight. Fog: — o o every two minutes.		

Sounds can be used to indicate what a vessel is about to do. You should have the equipment to make them on board.

One short blast	○	"I am turning to starboard".
Two short blasts	○ ○	"I am turning to port".
Three short blasts	○ ○ ○	"My engines are going astern" – this does not necessarily mean the craft is going backwards.
Five or more short blasts	○ ○ ○ ○ ○	"I don't understand your intentions" – perhaps better known as "What on earth are you doing?"

Traffic separation

Traffic separation schemes are denoted on a chart by purple shaded areas. Arrows on the chart denote the direction of the shipping lane. Traffic separation schemes separate large vessels in areas of heavy traffic. Always keep your vessel at right angles to the scheme so that you show the correct aspect to oncoming traffic.

17 | Buoyage

Two buoyage systems exist in the world, IALA A and IALA B. The difference affects the colour and light characteristics of lateral marks.

IALA A is used in Europe, Russia, India, Australia and New Zealand.

IALA B is used in the USA, South America and parts of the Caribbean, South East Asia and Canada.

Cardinals

Cardinal marks warn of danger and remain constant throughout the IALA system. The cones always point to the black bands.

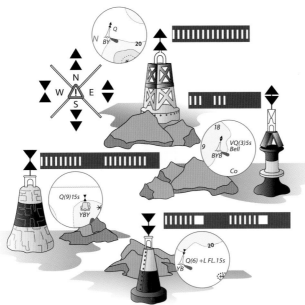

Other buoyage

Special Marks (yellow) can be used for a variety of reasons such as marking waterski areas, prohibited zones, racing marks, sewage outfalls and even wrecks. Isolated Danger buoys (black and red) typically mark areas of shallow water where all around is deep water whilst Fairway or Safewater Marks (white and red) identify areas where all around is deeper water – typically at the end of channels. Wreck Marks (yellow and blue) are a recent development and are laid temporarily to mark wrecks before either the wreck is lifted or marked on a more permanent basis.

IALA - A Buoyage Europe, Russia, India, Australia and New Zealand.

N

2 fixed greens

2 fixed reds

Fixed light
on breakwater

Isolated danger
If lit, always 2 flashes

Lesser channels
Often just posts some
with top marks

North Cardinal

Preferred channel
to starboard mark

Yellow special marks
have many uses from
dinghy racing marks to
outfall pipes and jet ski
areas. Often with an
X top mark - light flashing
yellow (any rhythm)

East Cardinal

South Cardinal

Cardinals sometimes
used to 'join' channels

Areas outside the main
channel are often
perfectly navigable
by small craft. Always
check your chart first for
hazards and available
depth

Lateral buoys
mark deep
water channels

West Cardinal indicates safe
water to west boundary of danger

Fairway buoy - safe water mark at
entrance to harbour or start of
buoyed channel
1 long white flash isophase, occulting
or morse A

5kt limit off beach marked by buoys
Boat lane to beach marked

Lateral marks

Used to mark channels.

In IALA A leave starboard cone to your
starboard side when going into harbour.

IALA - B Buoyage USA, South America and parts of the Caribbean, South East Asia and Canada.

N

2 fixed reds

2 fixed greens   Fixed light on breakwater

Isolated danger
If lit, always 2 flashes

Lesser channels
Often just posts some
with top marks

North Cardinal

Preferred channel
to starboard mark

Yellow special marks
have many uses from
dinghy racing marks to
outfall pipes and jet ski
areas. Often with an
X top mark - light flashing
yellow (any rhythm)

East Cardinal

South Cardinal

Cardinals sometimes
used to 'join' channels

Areas outside the main
channel are often
perfectly navigable
by small craft. Always
check your chart first for
hazards and available
depth

Lateral buoys
mark deep
water channels

West Cardinal indicates safe
water to west boundary of danger

Fairway buoy - safe water mark at
entrance to harbour or start of
buoyed channel
1 long white flash isophase, occulting
or morse A

5kt limit off beach marked by buoys
Boat lane to beach marked

PORT CAN
Flashes **GREEN** any rhythm
(except 2+1)

STARBOARD CONE
Flashes **RED** any rhythm
(except 2+1)

Lateral marks

Used to mark channels.

In IALA B leave starboard cone to your starboard side when going into harbour.

Navigation | 18

Navigation is the planning and execution of a passage between two points. Within this Chapter we will consider how we should plan then execute a passage but first we will look at the subjects such as charts and tides – subjects we should understand if we are to create safe and effective plans.

Charts

Charts are the nautical equivalent of road maps. They contain a wealth of valuable information and are an essential item for all craft.

As early explorers started to create maps of the world they soon needed to be able to define a precise position on the Earth's surface. To do this two sets of imaginary lines were 'drawn' on the Earth. One set of these lines runs North - South between the poles and are called meridians of longitude and the other set runs 'horizontally' around the Earth and are called parallels of latitude.

Longitude

Lines of longitude effectively divide the Earth into segments. Positions are referred to as either East or West of the Greenwich Meridian - the 000° line (eg: 030°W).

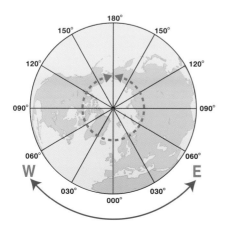

Looking down at the North Pole, the red line represents the 000° line of the Greenwich Meridian. The maximum value of longitude being 180°W or E.

Latitude

The parallel lines of latitude 'slice' the Earth into layers, any one of these lines of latitude can be defined by its angle relative to the equator - North or South. In this example 50°N. The maximum value of latitude being 90°N or S.

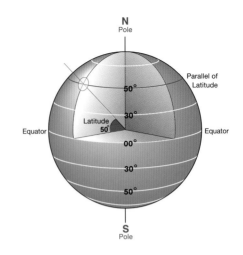

Therefore precise positions on the Earth's surface can be referred to by a line of latitude and a line of longitude.

A basic position can be defined as such:

50° 00'.0 N, 030° 00'.0 W

Each degree can be divided into fractions of a degree. Like hours, a degree consists of 60 minutes, and each minute consists of 60 seconds. Seconds are now usually expressed as decimals, so 002° 42' 30"W becomes 002° 42'.5W.

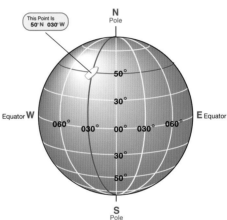

In the above example the craft is 50 degrees North (50°N), one degree of Latitude equals 60 nautical miles, therefore one minute of latitude equals one nautical mile (equals 1852m on land). So in this example 50° x 60 miles = 3000 miles north of the Equator.

Rarely though does a craft sit perfectly on such a precise position. For example a more typical position might be 53° 42'.5N, 001° 02'.5W. If relaying this position verbally you would say "Five three degrees four two decimal five minutes north, Zero zero one degrees zero two decimal five minutes west". Such clarity makes it easier for the other person to correctly hear the position, in a distress situation this could be critical.

Mercator projection

These early maps needed to transfer what appeared on the spherical earth to a flat sheet of paper. The method most commonly used is called Mercator's Projection. This can be visualised as the image that would be cast on a sheet of paper wrapped around the globe, with a bright light at the centre.

The compass

A compass allows you to:

- Steer on a particular heading.
- Take bearings of known objects and plot your position.
- Monitor the bearing to assess the risk of collision with other craft.

It is an essential item of safety and navigational kit. There are a variety of types of compass:

Traditional steering compass

- Should be mounted so that you can easily see it from the helm position.
- Ensure that the model you buy suits your boat.
- The compass consists of a card floating in liquid (to damp its movement) attached to a magnet.

GPS/Chartplotter Compass

- A screen found on most GPS/Chartplotter units.
- On most units the compass only works when the boat is moving. More expensive units may have a fluxgate compass built in so the compass works all of the time.

Fluxgate compass

- Electronic variant of the traditional compass.
- Able to pass steering information to other devices such as autopilots.
- Carefully follow the instructions to avoid creating errors during use.

Gyro Compass

- Usually the preserve of large ships and is highly accurate and stable.
- Cheaper Gyro compasses being used by small boats to great effect.
- Can be interfaced with autopilots.

A chart is only accurate on the day it is printed. Harbour authorities move, add or remove, buoys. Always check in the bottom left hand corner of the chart to see when it was last updated. Regular correction notices are published, and from these you should update your charts.

Correction notices are printed in many boating magazines and can now be downloaded from the chart manufacturer's website.

Chart - to plot position and course.

Logbook - records navigational information and ship's progress.

Almanac - gives tidal and pilotage data.

Streams atlas - gives information on tidal streams for an area.

Tidal Streams referred to at HW Strong Holm

Hours	Geographical Position	A 46°23'8N 6 00.0W			B 46°25'6N 5 46.7W			C 46°17'0N 5 58.2W			D 46°10'6N 5 53.9W			E 46°14'7N 5 52.3W			F 46°17'0N 5 47.3W		
-6		140	0.9	0.5	183	0.8	0.5	159	2.0	1.1	216	0.6	0.3	208	1.5	0.8	218	2.0	1.1
-5		139	0.3	0.1	178	0.4	0.2	157	1.1	0.6	003	0.8	0.4	106	0.8	0.5	216	1.0	0.5
-4		314	0.8	0.4	003	0.9	0.4	338	0.9	0.5	005	1.6	0.8	077	1.0	0.6	180	0.7	0.4
-3		317	1.8	0.9	005	1.7	0.9	336	2.1	1.1	008	2.1	1.0	071	1.8	1.0	042	1.1	0.6
-2		319	2.3	1.1	007	2.0	1.0	332	3.2	1.7	010	2.0	1.0	069	2.1	1.1	031	1.9	1.0
-1		322	1.5	0.7	004	1.6	0.8	327	1.8	0.9	012	1.7	0.8	068	1.7	0.9	028	2.2	1.2
High Water 0		324	1.0	0.5	003	1.1	0.6	327	1.8	0.9	014	1.2	0.7	068	1.7	0.9	025	1.8	0.9
+1		325	0.6	0.3	002	0.5	0.3	325	1.2	0.7	016	1.0	0.6	095	1.0	0.6	004	0.9	0.5
+2		142	0.5	0.3	179	0.6	0.4	152	1.7	0.8	199	1.0	0.5	183	1.0	0.6	223	1.2	0.7
+3		141	1.7	0.7	180	1.6	0.8	154	2.2	1.2	208	1.4	0.7	192	1.8	1.0	221	1.9	1.0
+4		139	2.4	1.1	181	2.2	1.2	155	2.6	1.4	210	1.9	1.0	195	2.0	1.1	221	2.2	1.2
+5		138	2.1	1.0	182	1.9	1.0	157	2.4	1.3	212	1.7	0.8	198	1.7	0.9	219	2.1	1.2
+6		140	1.6	0.7	184	1.4	0.7	159	2.1	1.1	214	0.9	0.5	201	1.6	0.8	218	2.0	1.1

Left-hand labels: Before High Water / After High Water — Directions of streams (degrees) — Rates at spring tides (knots) — Rates at neap tides (knots)

Latitude scale - use this for measuring distance.

A key to chart symbols can be found in publication Symbols and Abbreviations.

The Edition date lets you check with a chart list to see if you have the latest edition (although most charts are not updated every year).

Chart corrections are listed here.

NOT TO BE USED FOR NAVIGATION

Customer Information
Edition Number: 1
Edition Date: 2nd March 2006

Notices to Mariners 2006

nonds give set
of tidal streams.

Compass rose also
gives magnetic variation.

Chart title - describes
area covered.

Scale: 1 unit of distance on this
chart = (in this case) 30,000
units on the earth's surface.

Other important information and
any warnings are given here.

Longitude scale - used
for position only, NOT
for measuring distance.

Chart catalogue
number.

WGS84 POSITIONS
can be plotted directly on this chart

RYA4

Range and bearing on a chart

You can use a plotting instrument to measure the bearing from one object to another on a chart. This could be used to navigate between these two points or to describe the position of one object relative to the other. Position plotting instrument, rotate centre to align green arrows to north, read off bearing.

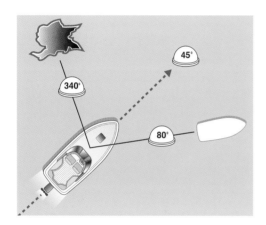

In this example the powerboat's heading is 045°, the bearing of the craft to starboard is 080° and the rock to port is 340°.

Measuring distance on a chart

When measuring distance, always take the dividers to the 'latitude' scale on the side of the chart alongside the area that you are measuring.

Remember one minute of latitude equals one nautical mile.

Plotting a Position

To plot a position on a chart from a latitude and longitude:

- Mark off the latitude by marking a line from the vertical scale in the area you expect it to intersect the meridian of longitude.

- Mark off the meridian of longitude from the horizontal scale at the top or bottom of the chart.
- Where the lines intersect is the position.

Tip - When plotting you can either use a plotter or dividers. A plotter is easier on a small powerboat.

Tip - Your thumb and forefinger make a great set of dividers whilst the side of your hand when laid on a chart is not bad as a plotting tool. Sometimes a quick approach works just fine in a small boat.

Variation

A compass points to Magnetic North rather than to the North Pole. On a chart, the vertical lines point to 'True' North.

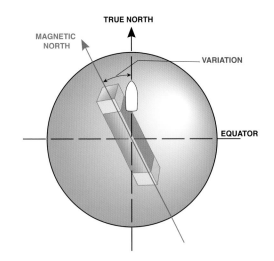

This difference between True and Magnetic North is called variation. When transferring bearings from a chart to use on a compass, they need to be converted from True to Magnetic. Likewise, when reading bearings from a compass they need converting before plotting on a chart.

Adjusting for variation

True to magnetic: Add variation if west, subtract if east

For example:

If True (T) course = 107°
and Variation (V) = 4°W

then Magnetic (M) = 107°T + 4°W = 111°M

Magnetic to true: Subtract variation if west, add if east

True = 111°M − 4°W (V) = 107°T

Variation was 6° 40′W in 2004 changing by 8′ E per annum

Variation can vary greatly between different boating areas, and changes over time. It is calculated and recorded on charts.

In the example in the image what would the variation be in 2010 - 6 years after the variation shown in the compass rose was calculated?

Variation is shown as changing by 8'E per annum. 6 years multiplied by 8' is 48'E. Variation was 6° 40'W so will have reduced by 48' as the change is E, so in 2010 the updated variation is 5° 52'W. In practice this is pretty much 6° or in smaller boats with less accurate compasses assume 5°.

Deviation

Deviation is the error caused by metal items (or electronic fields) on board affecting the compass reading. The error varies as the heading changes. To properly allow for deviation, a deviation card detailing the error at each heading is required.

The simplest way to create a deviation card is to compare the reading from the steering compass with the reading from a hand-bearing compass, which is held well clear of any possible interference. Do this for various headings, and then plot the errors to create your own deviation card. Alternatively a compass adjuster can swing the compass and create a card for you.

To adjust from Magnetic to Compass
(i.e. to adjust for deviation)

C = M + Westerly deviation

C = M – Easterly deviation

To adjust Compass to Magnetic

M = C – Westerly deviation

M = C + Easterly deviation

In the example from the previous page, when the Magnetic heading is 111°M, the deviation table shows a deviation of about 5° E. Using C = M – Easterly deviation gives 111°M – 5° E = 106°C.

The compass heading (C) will be 106°C.

Tip - Remembering all these adjustments is not easy. In your boating area variation will probably always be either W or E, so just remember one of the equations, e.g., 'M = T + West Variation'. Deviation is then applied to the result and is vessel specific.

Tides and tidal streams

The gravitational effect of the Moon and Sun on the Earth are the main cause of tides.

Spring tides When the Earth is in line with the Moon and Sun, high tides are at their highest, and low tides at their lowest.

Neap tides When the Earth, Moon and Sun are not in alignment high and low tides are smaller than spring tides.

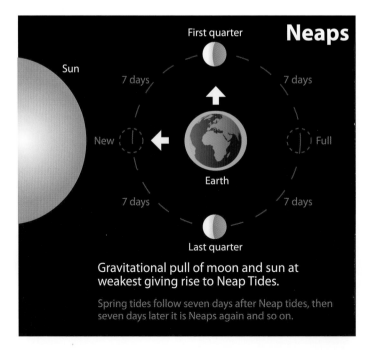

Charts are drawn to the lowest possible tide ever likely to be experienced at that point – the Lowest Astronomical Tide. This level is known as Chart Datum, below this level Charted Depths are measured and above are Drying Heights.

The height of tide is added to these figures to calculate the depth of water at that point.

'A' is a charted depth. For example, if this charted depth was 2.4m and you know the height of tide will be 0.8m, then the depth at that point is 2.4m + 0.8m = 3.2m. 'B' is a drying height, meaning this area is exposed at the Lowest Astronomical Tide. Imagine the chart showed 0.3m as the drying height. If the tide was 0.8m then there would be 0.5m of water present above this area at this tidal height (0.8m - 0.3m).

In most places high tides follow low tides on a roughly six hour cycle (i.e., two highs and two lows per day). Springs and neaps alternate on a seven day cycle.

Tidal information is available from a variety of sources:

- Nautical almanacs contain a wealth of information. Tidal data is shown in a table with the times of high water, low water, and the tidal height. Use this with the tidal curve for any location to calculate tidal heights at any time.

- Local tide tables/curves: Increasingly popular are the tidal curve booklets available for local areas. These are easy to use.

- The Internet.

Tip - It's very easy to pick the wrong day or forget the correction for summertime so when you have gathered your tidal information always double check. Is the level of tide that you see on arrival at your launch site or marina the same as the almanac?

Note - Highest Astronomical Tide ('HAT') is replacing MHWS as the reference level for the heights of objects – such as the underside of bridges or lighthouses. Be careful to check your chart and almanac to see which is being used.

Tidal streams

Knowing the rate and direction of flow at a given time is important because:

- You can make your passage with the stream rather than push against it to give a faster passage.

- You can time your passage to avoid a dangerous situation, such as where wind is opposing stream making rougher water.

Tidal stream data is available in two forms:

Tidal stream atlas

Tidal stream maps are found in almanacs and tidal stream atlases. These show the direction and rate of the tide at hour intervals before and after high water. The figures (11,20) mean that the rate at neaps is 1.1 knots, while at springs (which is usually greater) it is 2.0 knots. The direction of the arrow gives the direction of flow.

If between springs and neaps, it is usual to interpolate to achieve the correct figure.

Tidal diamonds

Tidal diamonds are found on charts. The figures which relate to these diamonds are found elsewhere on the chart and show the rate and direction of the tide at springs and neaps.

Tip - When the direction of a tide is quoted (e.g. 090°) this is the direction the tide flows towards.

Tidal curves

If you want to know the tidal height between the times of high and low water you can use a tidal curve to calculate the tidal height at any time.

A tidal curve shows how the tide varies between high and low water. They are found in almanacs for major boating locations.

To use a tidal curve:

- Find the tidal data from the almanac for the day concerned. The almanac will tell you which 'Standard port' and curve to use for your location – in this case Dover.

- Adjust high water time to Daylight Saving Time (if required) and enter it in box (A). In this example HW is at 1300 DST.

- Fill in the remaining boxes in one hour increments either side of HW.

- Mark the HW and LW tidal heights onto the graph (B) and connect them with a line (C).

- Calculate the 'tidal range' (difference in height between HW and LW), by subtracting the LW height from the HW height. A small box on the curve indicates which curve line to use. In this example 6.8m – 0.6m = 6.2m range. 6.2 range = springs, therefore the solid curve line (red) is used.

You can now use the curve to calculate the tidal heights from the curve.

Example:

- To find the tidal height at 10.30am, draw a vertical line (Line D) from the 10.30 time until it intersects the curve. Then run the line to the diagonal depth line and up to read off the height. It reads as 3.6m.

- To find when the tidal height will be 5.0m. Draw a vertical line from the tidal height scale (E) down to the diagonal line, then across to the curve.

- The two points either side, where it bisects the curve, will give you the times when the height is 5.0m. At any time between these times the tide is in excess of this height. The times read as between about 1110 and 1540.

Rule of Twelfths

If you want to know the tidal height at a given time but do not have a tidal curve to hand, you can approximate roughly using the rule of twelfths. The rule assumes that the rise and fall of tide is symmetrical and occurs every six hours.

This rule suggests:

- 1st hour – 1/12th of tide rises or falls
- 2nd hour – 2/12ths of tide rises or falls
- 3rd hour – 3/12ths of tide rises or falls
- 4th hour – 3/12ths of tide rises or falls
- 5th hour – 2/12ths of tide rises or falls
- 6th hour – 1/12th of tide rises or falls

For example:

HW = 4.8m at 0600.

LW = 1.2m at 1200.

What is the tidal height at 1100?

- The range is 3.6m (4.8m – 1.2m).
- 1100 is 1 hour before low water.
- The fall of the tide in the last hour is 1/12th x 3.6m = 0.3m.
- So 1 hour before low water the tidal height will be 0.3m + 1.2m = 1.5m.

What the rule of twelfths also graphically illustrates is that far more tide flows in the 3rd and 4th hours than at other times, therefore the tidal rate is also greater.

However, the rule of twelfths doesn't apply in every location.

> **Tip** - Remember the tidal height is not the depth of water. Add it to the figures on the chart to calculate the depth at that point.
>
> **Tip** - Some areas have unusual tidal characteristics and the tidal curves may be drawn around low water.

Passage planning and pilotage

Passage planning: Is the preparation of a plan that helps you safely navigate between two areas and normally relates to passages at sea.

Pilotage: Is what you do at either end of your passage and is inshore navigation using buoyage, depth, lights, transits and other techniques to safely manoeuvre your craft along the coast and into or out of a harbour or marina.

Where you are going will define what will be in your plan and how you 'record' it. A skipper undertaking a passage needs to consider a variety of factors:

Weather

- What is it doing now and how will it change over the duration of the passage.
- How will it affect your passage (e.g. wind against stream)?
- Can you regularly update weather information during the journey.

The route

- Have charts of a suitable scale for the route and harbours that will, or may be, entered.
- Create the route and document headings, waypoints, distances, times, speeds, depths etc.
- Record dangerous, key or useful features on route.

Tidal heights and streams

- Is there enough water to enter and exit the harbour and undertake the passage?
- When should the passage commence to avoid unfavourable conditions (e.g. wind against stream) and to ensure safe entry to the destination port.

Pilotage

- Plan harbour entry or exits, note important features such as marks and lights.
- Repeat for ports of refuge.

There are many ways to record a passage plan and a skipper must make a judgement call as to what approach best suits the passage being made. A short trip to a local bay is technically a passage but does not necessarily require a written plan if thought has gone into the passage. A 15 mile trip along the coast though would benefit from a fairly detailed (but simple) document addressing all of the above.

> **Tip** - A responsible skipper ensures that someone (be it the Coastguard or a friend) knows where he intends going and when he should be there.

Pilotage

In smaller craft most passages occur in congested inshore waters where there are numerous hazards but also plenty of visual references to help you keep your boat on its intended route.

The best way to do this is to study a chart and almanac to create a Pilotage Plan containing the key details of your route.

This Pilotage Plan should be used alongside a chart which you annotate with the details of your intended track so that you can quickly refer between your plan and the chart.

Pilotage techniques

There are various techniques that can be used for pilotage.

Transits Line up two charted objects to keep you on your intended track.

(B) = To port

On course

(A) = To starboard

Bearing and distance Know the heading and distance between charted objects then steer to this heading. Keeping a certain speed gives a predicted time for the leg but be careful as small errors in heading can lead to large errors in position even over fairly short legs – use in conjunction with one of the other techniques detailed here.

Clearing lines & bearings Use clearing lines or clearing bearings to define areas of safety and danger. These are easy to use afloat once calculated.

Back bearings Calculate bearings to known objects allowing you to steer away from a known object on a heading checking the back bearing to ensure you remain on the track you want.

Turning points Calculate turning points by reference to bearings to known objects or transits between two points.

Depth and Contour lines Knowing the depth you expect to see on your depth gauge gives you a good indication of whether you are in the area you expect to be, calculate expected depth on contour lines and use these to navigate along or fix position with.

GPS Waypoints & routes (see page 106) You can enter waypoints and create routes and use various GPS based techniques to help you navigate along your intended track.

Fixing your position

A good Skipper knows at all times where he is and regularly plots his position on a chart.

Visually Keep it simple, if you are near a charted object then you know exactly where you are. Be sure it is the one you think it is though!

Bearing and contours As you cross a contour line take a bearing to a charted object. A transit and a contour line would be even more accurate.

Craft takes bearing and skipper knows he must be on this line
Calculate depth to work out where craft is on line

Transit and bearing Ideally choose an object at roughly right angles to the transit for the best fix.

Radar ranges Use the *Variable Range Marker* ring to select 2 or 3 charted objects for a very precise fix.

Compass used to plot range from arrowed points

Radar bearings Another method using radar is to fix with 3 radar bearings or a mix of bearings and contours/transits etc. Beware though as there can be errors due to the way the radar beam appears to stretch objects making the bearings produced not entirely accurate.

Bearing taken using Electronic Bearing Line (EBL).
Radar tends to show targets elongated.
Plot position of craft using 3 Point Fix method.

3 point fix

- Look for easily identifiable positions on the chart and ashore.

- Ensure they are 50-100° apart to achieve a good cut.

- Note down the bearings and the time and log reading.

- Convert the bearings to 'true' and plot them.

- Where they cross is your position - mark time and log on the chart.

- Double check this by other means – depth or a good look around.

- A 'Cocked Hat' is where you have a triangle of intersection.

- The position is historical and refers to a particular time and log reading.

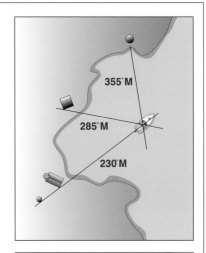

Estimated position The same principles can be used to estimate where you are or where you will end up. The terms used are 'dead reckoning' (DR) and 'estimated position' (EP).

For example, a craft achieves 15 knots on a heading of 080°T. Plot the line on a chart depicting the water track. The point on the line that the craft has reached after a certain period of time is its position – this is dead reckoning. It may not be very accurate as it ignores stream. Add in the tidal vector for the same time period for a far more accurate estimate – your estimated position. This can be repeated for different speeds, headings and tidal streams to represent your journey.

Using GPS/Chartplotters With a basic GPS just displaying latitude and longitude then either plot the position on the chart or use the GPS based techniques discussed later in the chapter. If using a chartplotter then it may be the image shown on the plotter allows you to simply transfer a position to a chart.

Hand-bearing compass

An essential item for good pilotage. Can be used:

- To take bearings, back bearings, 3 point fixes etc.
- To take relative bearings in potential collision situations.
- To check the main steering compass.

Course to Steer

In some areas a simple course can be laid on the chart and that course steered. In areas where there is stream things are different. If the boat heads directly at the target point, the stream may push it off the track. In this case a compensation for this effect is made by altering the heading.

To calculate to allow for a cross stream and find what the revised heading should be:

- Draw a line from A through B and beyond.
- This is the Ground Track (two arrows denotes Ground Track).
- From A plot the 'Tidal Vector' (three arrows). In this case the Tidal Rate is 170°T 1.3 knots so plot 1.3M.

- Open the dividers to the distance the craft would travel in 1 hour.
- This craft at 5 knots would travel 5 miles in 1 hour.
- Mark off where the dividers intersect the line A-B making point C.
- Join these two points, this is the water track (1 arrow).

Note - A common mistake is to join the end of the tidal vector and point B instead of using dividers to measure distance travelled in one hour.

- Read the angle of the water track.
- This is the 'Course to Steer'.
- This will need adjusting for Variation and Deviation to give Compass.
- The distance A-C is the actual distance the craft will travel in 1 hour.
- This is the 'Speed Over Ground'.

In this example the size of the vector diagram fits comfortably onto the chart. The diagram can be plotted over a 30 minute period rather than an hour, as shown, if that fits better, e.g., plot a half hour ground track, a half hour tidal vector, and so on.

Tip - If you are undertaking a long passage, the rate and direction of the tide will vary often. In this case you can undertake a series of these calculations for each hour of the journey – do not assume that the tide direction and rate will remain constant during the passage.

Leeway

Leeway is the effect the wind has on a craft. At speed, powerboats are affected far less by the wind than yachts or slower motorboats. High sided craft in windy conditions may need to adjust for leeway. If wind is blowing on your beam, assume that you need to adjust by 5° or 10° by altering your heading to steer more into the wind. If the wind increases you may need to allow for more leeway.

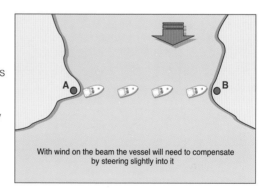

With wind on the beam the vessel will need to compensate by steering slightly into it

Chartwork

Chartwork allows us to work out our intended passage or where we should be from where we have been. We use plotting symbols on the chart to make it easy to follow.

⊙	Fix		Fix obtained by ranges
△	Estimated position		
	Dead reckoning position	→	Water track
⊕	Waypoint (WPT)	⇒	Ground track
	Fix from visual bearings	⇛	Tidal set and drift

Electronic navigation

The GPS (Global Positioning System) has become the centre piece of most boaters' navigation 'toolbox'.

Used effectively electronic navigation can be the primary means of navigation but should be backed up by traditional navigation methods.

GPS receivers calculate their position by reference to a number of satellites that orbit the Earth. Receivers come in many shapes, from small hand-held units to the large permanently fixed sets built into many boats. They are typically accurate to between 10m and 15m and because they know where you are and where you were they can calculate the boat's speed and course over the ground.

The majority of sets used on craft nowadays are chartplotters. These GPS units have electronic charts either programmed in to the unit or on a separate data card and display the position of the vessel on the chart.

Advantages:

- The boat is graphically displayed on a chart for instant position information.

- Waypoints and routes are easy to plot and check for accuracy. The safety of your route can be assessed quickly.

- The chart can be zoomed in on and extra detail added or removed according to need.

- A small data card can hold a considerable number of charts.

Disadvantages:

- Like anything electronic they can fail – electronic charts should be used alongside paper charts.

- To update the chart you need to reprogram the data card – this should be done annually.

- Screen size is important as it allows the 'bigger picture' to be viewed. Large screens can be expensive.

The smaller GPS units that display just latitude and longitude and don't include built in charts are powerful navigational tools too though and many boaters carry them either instead of a chartplotter or as a backup to a fixed set.

Waypoints and routes

A waypoint is a predetermined point along an intended track. The set will calculate the distance and bearing from its current position to give a course to the waypoint. Once the vessel starts to move to the waypoint, it will also calculate the estimated time of arrival at the waypoint and whether the boat is straying either side of the direct course line.

- Waypoints can be entered either using a cursor on the chart (with a chartplotter) or directly entered as a latitude and longitude.

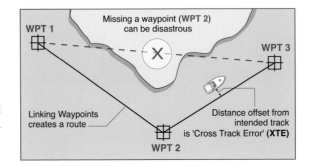

- Waypoints can be linked together to form a route.

- Ensure waypoints and routes do not take the vessel into danger.

- Plot your intended route on a chart and double check the bearing and distance according to the GPS unit.

- Ensure that the GPS receiver is set to the same geodetic datum as the chart

- The compass display will only work when the set is moving – unless the set has an inbuilt fluxgate compass.

- Keep a log of your position so that in the event of failure of your electronics you know where you are.

Over time different assumptions have been made about where the centre of the Earth is. This affects where the lines of latitude and longitude are drawn. Newer charts are drawn to the WGS84 geodetic datum whereas older charts might be drawn to the OSGB36 datum or assumption. Ensure your GPS is set to the same datum as your chart or you might need to make adjustments when you plot.

Steering to a waypoint

A GPS usually has a few different screens that can be used to steer to a waypoint. The usual screens are a 'rolling road' or a compass needle that points in the required direction.

Remember with waypoints:

• Steering to a single waypoint doesn't usually allow for tide so you may be pushed off your intended track. Join waypoints to navigate along a route in preference to using individual waypoints.

• Place waypoints adjacent to charted objects to lessen the chance of hitting them.

• In busy areas many craft may choose the same waypoint – enter your own distinct waypoint for safety.

• Electronics can fail so know where you are on your chart and know how to use traditional navigational techniques.

Cross track error, or XTE

The problem with straying off the intended track is that danger may lurk off the direct line. Straying either side of the line is called 'cross track error' (XTE) and an alarm can be set after deciding an acceptable XTE for your route. The term 'Off Course' is used by some manufacturers in preference to XTE.

Using a GPS unit for navigation

A variety of techniques have evolved to make the most out of GPS based navigation. Some of these techniques can be used both to navigate between two points or as a means of fixing your position.

Waypoint web Plot a waypoint on the chart - 'C'. From the waypoint, draw a series of lines at different bearings and use compasses to draw arcs of distance from the waypoint. Then as you head towards that waypoint, it is easy to read off the distance and bearing of the waypoint and plot your position on the 'web'. This technique is very useful at night or in rougher conditions and works equally well whether you are navigating towards the waypoint C or simply across the area covered by the web.

Compass rose waypoint An adaptation of this is to use a compass rose on a chart. Enter a waypoint at the centre of the compass rose, select 'goto' that waypoint. The GPS will then tell you the bearing and distance to that waypoint. You can now plot your position easily and accurately onto the chart using the compass rose to help you plot. Check to ensure the GPS is configured to give the bearing in true or remember to adjust for variation.

Waypoint ladder To create a waypoint ladder simply draw a line between two waypoints and mark off 0.5 or 1M intervals to form a ladder. When running between the waypoints you can read off distance and XTE from the GPS unit and easily plot your position alongside the ladder or gauge your position by eye.

Radar

Radar works by sending out radio waves that rebound off a solid object, back to the radar. These radio echoes are then displayed on a screen. The size and strength of the echo depends on what is reflected. A tanker will give a better echo than a small wooden sailing boat.

To increase a small boat's echo, radar reflectors are placed on the flybridge or deck head to amplify the signal return. Even if radar is fitted, a reflector is still required.

Radar is now fitted into a growing number of smaller boats. Radar and chart plotter systems can be integrated to display on the same screen. The images can be overlaid or viewed as separate screens. They are excellent for use at night and in restricted visibility. However, bear in mind:

- Radar is not as intuitive as a chart plotter or GPS. Taking a training course to understand their use is a good idea.

- The ability to interpret what you see grows with experience. Practise in good conditions before you use the system for real.

- Radar can display the picture in 'North-up', 'Course-up', or 'Head-up' mode. Make sure that you know what you are looking at.

- This radar screen and chart are depicting the same area. The radar is in 'Course-up', the chart is in 'North-up'.

19 | Weather

Weather plays a fundamental role in your decision whether to go to sea. Being able to assess the weather conditions you may encounter during the intended passage is a basic requirement of a skipper. With experience you are able to read a weather forecast and make a judgement based on it.

Causes of weather

The weather systems that we experience are caused by the movement of air created by the warming of the Earth. Hot air at the Equator rises and is replaced by cooler air moving in from elsewhere. The irregular distribution of land and water masses create a pattern of hot and cold areas producing bands of high and low pressure like corridors around the Earth.

Spinning of the Earth allows these highs and lows to move, collide and mix with each other causing weather systems.

These weather systems give rise to areas of high and low pressure.

Depression or 'Low'

Anticyclone or 'High'

- Unsettled weather

- Rainfall – often heavy

- Strong winds pointing towards centre – anticlockwise northern hemisphere, clockwise southern hemisphere

- A general direction of travel from west to east

- Closely spaced isobars

- Good settled weather

- Clear skies

- Light winds point away from centre - clockwise northern hemisphere, anticlockwise southern hemisphere

- Widely spaced isobars

It is the 'Depressions' or 'Lows' that we need to be most careful of and aware of when we go afloat.

The progression of a depression

The depression is passing from west to east; the warm front appears first, followed by the cold front. In some areas, especially in the Southern Hemisphere, the warm front is hardly noticed but the cold front brings worsening weather.

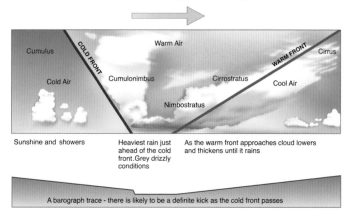

Sunshine and showers | Heaviest rain just ahead of the cold front.Grey drizzly conditions | As the warm front approaches cloud lowers and thickens until it rains

A barograph trace - there is likely to be a definite kick as the cold front passes

Barometer readings as fronts pass

Types of cloud in a depression				
Cumulus	Low cloud and rain	Altostratus thickening to nimbostratus	Cirrostratus	High cirrus cloud
As the cold front arrives, the pressure can drop again. There may be heavy rain, strong winds and perhaps thunderstorms. The cloud is cumulus or cumulonimbus.	In the warm sector, the barometer stops falling. The rain either ceases or eases but the cloud base is low with poor visibility.	The cloud continues to thicken becoming nimbostratus and the cloud level has lowered. As the front approaches it begins to rain.	The cloud has thickened into cirrostratus and the barometer continues to fall. The wind direction 'backs' (moves anticlockwise) often from a SW direction to southerly.	The high, thin cirrus clouds indicate the approach of a depression (12–24 hours away). The barometer starts to fall.

Tip - The way pressure is rising or falling can tell you much about the likely weather to follow. Rapidly falling or rising pressure indicates very unsettled weather ahead. A rise or fall of 4mb within three hours usually indicates strong winds, and a change of 6mb indicates a possible gale.

Sea breezes

Sea breezes are caused by the flow of air from the sea to the land to fill the void created by the rising of hot air as it is warmed over land. Sea breezes occur in the afternoon on clear, hot sunny days. They always blow onshore and their strength can be increased or decreased by the actual wind direction.

Early stages of sea breeze developing. Heat rising over the land is creating the line of clouds

Fog

Being caught in fog can be a very frightening and dangerous experience for a boater. The most common types of fog are caused by the cooling of the air to a point where moisture in the air condenses into droplets.

The three main types of fog are:

- **Radiation fog**   - this tends to occur overnight and disperses rapidly as the ground warms. Caused by the rapidly cooling land where a warm, moist airstream exists.

- **Advection fog**   - caused by the passage of warm moist air over the cold water. Requires a drier airstream to clear it – also known as 'Sea fog'.

- **Frontal fog**   - may occur at a warm front, and tends not to persist. Caused by warm air rising over cold air.

Interpreting weather information

As Skipper you need to gather weather information and then make an informed decision whether it is safe to undertake the trip that you have planned. Make sure before you finally go afloat you have assessed the most recent forecast.

On most weather websites you can view detailed national weather forecasts like 'The Shipping Forecast', more detailed local forecasts like the 'Inshore Waters Forecast' and the Weather Maps from which these forecasts are compiled. Particular words and phrases are used in some of these forecasts to indicate certain conditions and you need to understand this 'language' to be able to properly interpret these forecasts.

Interpreting a weather map

Key points to help you interpret a weather chart include:

- The lines on a weather chart join areas of equal pressure – these are called isobars.
- The closer these lines are together the greater the pressure gradient and the greater the wind speed.
- At the intersections of high and low pressure systems the rotation of the wind may combine to create wind speeds greater than implied by the isobar spacing. Adjacent low pressure systems may create the opposite effect with winds being lower than implied by the spacing.
- Weather maps often contain a wind speed key (top left hand corner of this map) – at your latitude use the scale to estimate the wind speed from the isobar spacing.
- In the area shown on the map depressions will tend to move north easterly.

Sourcing weather forecasts

There are a variety of sources of weather forecasts and weather data that you can use:

The Internet	An increasingly popular source of forecasts with a wealth of data. Some weather files can even be downloaded and overlaid onto to a Navigation computer screen.
National and local radio	Many countries give a national shipping forecast that gives reasonable information but many tend to be too generalised and lack specific local information. Local radio stations near boating areas often broadcast excellent local forecasts.
VHF	Coastguard stations usually broadcast regular weather forecasts on the VHF radio. These forecasts often cover very specific areas and are extremely useful. Some areas of the world use VHF weather channels that continuously broadcast the current forecast.
Commercial services	Commercial forecasting services offer a phone/fax/sms service with both the national forecast and local forecasts.
Marinas and harbour masters	Can generally be relied upon to post copies of the inshore waters forecast alongside a weather chart for the day.
Newspapers and television	Local TV stations often broadcast reasonable data. However, forecasts on the national news are usually too general. Local newspapers can be useful but may lack detail.
Navtex	A radio receiver mainly fitted to larger craft, but also found in marinas; prints or displays weather forecasts and general safety broadcasts.

The Beaufort Scale

Force	Wind speed	Description	Wave height	Sea state
0	< 1 knot	Calm	0m	Mirror like
1	1–3 knots	Light air	Up to 0.1m	Ripples on the surface
2	4–6 knots	Light breeze	Up to 0.3m	Small wavelets with smooth crests
3	7–10 knots	Gentle breeze	Up to 0.9m	Large wavelets with crests starting to break
4	11–16 knots	Moderate breeze	Up to 1.5m	Large waves begin to form with white foam crests
5	17–21 knots	Fresh breeze	Up to 2.5m	Moderate waves and many white horses
6	22–27 knots	Strong breeze	Up to 4m	Large waves, spray and white foam crests
7	28–33 knots	Near gale	Up to 5.5m	Breaking waves, a heaped sea, lots of spray
8	34–40 knots	Gale	Up to 7.5m	Frequently breaking, moderately high waves
9	41–47 knots	Severe gale	Up to 10m	High waves, flying spray and breaking crests
10	48–55 knots	Storm	Up to 12.5m	Very high waves, almost totally white, with foam and spray
11	56–63 knots	Violent storm	Up to 16m	Extensive foam, exceptionally high waves, visibility seriously affected
12	> 64 knots	Hurricane	16m +	Air filled with foam and spray, very poor visibility

Tip - A fairly easy to handle Force 4 for one craft may be the equivalent of storm force to another. Beware of and understand your vessel's limitations and that of its crew.

Developing the skills needed to interpret forecasts and predict weather takes time. One of the best ways to develop your capability is to listen to and read forecasts. Develop an understanding of different weather systems and continually compare what you see and experience with the forecasts.

20 | Boating at Night and in Restricted Visibility

What is a quite straightforward area to cruise during the day takes on a very different outlook after dark. Boating at night is usually planned but sometimes becomes necessary because of a delayed schedule or some other problem. Good preparation is the key.

Boating at night is very different than during the day, the visual information available to you needs interpreting and if you fail to plan you are very likely to make potentially dangerous errors. To put a plan together for entry into a port or harbour study the relevant chart and almanac noting the key features that are likely to be visible at night, these might include:

- Lit buoys – laterals, cardinals and other buoyage
- Sectored, directional and leading lights
- Lights on chimneys, radios masts, tall buildings

Use this information to draw up a pilotage plan similar to those used in daylight ensuring the features you note are visible at night in some way. Note too the areas of danger – unlit marks, shallow areas, moorings. Do not use buildings or lights ashore unless you are 100% sure they will be visible and identifiable at night.

A plan for a night passage could look something like this:

Pilotage techniques at night include:

Transits Line up two lights to use as a heading to follow or to identify turn points. These are known as 'leading lights'.

Clearing lines Like during daylight use these to identify areas of danger or safe water.

Back bearings Calculate bearings from very obvious lit objects – buoys, lights on chimneys. Distinctive lights like a 'Quick Red' (QR) will be easier to use than one that flashes intermittently.

Turning points Calculate turning points by reference to bearings to known objects or use transits or leading lights.

Bearing and distance Know the heading and distance between charted objects then steer to this heading – over distance small errors in heading can lead to larger errors in position though.

Using waypoints and routes at night is an valid technique, don't forget to keep a good lookout though. Your depth sounder works equally well in the dark too.

Sectored lights

Sectored lights assist you to avoid danger by casting a coloured light over an area of danger.

Directional lights

These assist entry to a harbour by identifying the safest approach.

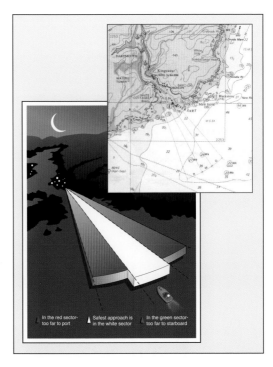

Remember:

- Wear lifejackets and ensure that they have lights fitted.
- Ensure you have warm clothing available – it can be far colder at night.
- Prepare the boat and crew: Dim the instrument and equipment lights to preserve night vision, use red lights where possible or filters to preserve night vision.
- Have torches available for reading charts – ideally with red filters.
- Maintain a good lookout and be especially aware of lobster pot markers and unlit buoys.
- If on a passage, plan a watch system.
- Always have a plan 'B' – and an all weather port of refuge available.
- When 'buoy hopping' at night never drive directly at the buoy, choose a point offset well to one side – staying away from hard objects always makes sense!
- Ensure you always know where you are and can plot the position on a chart using the techniques already identified adapted for night use.

Position fixing at night

In addition to the Position Fixing techniques already identified in Chapter 18 which can be adapted to work at night, you can also fix your position using the intersection of the lights from Sectored Lights and Directional Lights in combination with bearings, contours or transits.

A combination of the pilotage techniques identified can be used to safely find unlit marks at night if the need arises.

Light sequences

Light Symbols on a chart refer to the way in which the light on a buoy flashes. The commonest types are:

NAME	CHART SYMBOL	DESCRIPTION	VISUALLY
Fixed	F	Fixed light - always on	
Flashing	Fl	Flashing, off more than on	
Group flashing	Fl (2)	Flashing in groups	
Long flashing	LFl	Flashing, off more than on but on lasting 2 or more seconds	
Quick	Q	50 - 79 flashes per min	
Very quick	VQ	80 - 90 flashes per min	
Group quick	Q (9)	A group of quick flashes followed by a period off	
Interrupted quick	IQ	Similar to group quick but with no specified number of flashes	
Isophase	Iso	Equally on and off	
Occulting	Oc	More on than off	
Alternating	Al.WR	Colour changes	
Fixed and flashing	F Fl(2)	Fixed light with flashes at higher intensity	

Restricted visibility

Boating in fog can be one of the most dangerous situations for a small craft.

If fog is predicted, going to sea is foolhardy and should be avoided. If you are already at sea when fog descends, the safe option is to turn back and return to port or, if that is not a safe option, make way to a safe area away from shipping. Either way, as Skipper your first responsibility is for your crew, and your actions should reflect this.

If you are already at sea

- Reduce speed to just a few knots.
- Confirm your position.
- All crew should wear lifejackets.
- Hoist a radar reflector.
- Switch on navigation lights.
- Sound the appropriate sound signal – usually 1 long blast every two minutes.
- Post a crew member to listen and look for other craft.
- Consider switching off the engine every few minutes to hear other craft.
- Confirm your position.
- If you are in a shipping lane or main channel, move to shallow water.
- Consider anchoring in shallow water until the fog lifts.

Whether or not you make a 'run for home' will be influenced by a variety of factors: where you are; your navigation skills; whether you possess a radar or chart plotter and the knowledge to competently use them; and how easy is the entry into the harbour. If you do decide to enter a harbour or marina, create a plan containing the information you will need to make a safe entry.

Tip - It is good practice to pre-enter your GPS with waypoints and routes into harbours you will pass by to act as 'ports of refuge' in the event of a problem.

Trailing Your Boat

Trailing a boat can be a stressful, tiring experience or relatively straightforward – the difference is preparation.

Secure all equipment before trailing

Key points to remember are:

- Ensure your tow vehicle is up to the job. The combined weight of the trailer and boat should not exceed the permissible towing limit for the vehicle.

- Ensure the vehicle is capable of pulling the trailer up the slipways you intend using.

- In most situations if the combined weight of boat and trailer exceeds 750kg, the trailer needs to be fitted with brakes.

- Regularly grease and oil the trailer as necessary. Ensure wheel bearings are regularly repacked with fresh grease to enhance their life.

- Ensure that the trailer is set up for the boat it is to carry. See that rollers are well positioned and the transom of the boat, which carries the weight of the engine through to the trailer, is supported and does not overhang the rollers by more than about 50cm.

- When towing, tie the boat down to the trailer tightly. Any movement between the two can cause a lot of damage.

- Never immerse a trailer with hot wheel bearings into cold water, or the bearings will lose their grease and fail. Allow the bearings to cool for 45 minutes after a trip.

- Fit a safety chain or rope between the trailer and the tow vehicle so that if the trailer breaks away it will stay with the tow vehicle.

- Carry a spare wheel and all the tools you will need to change it.

Trailing checklist

Going overseas

One of the great advantages of a boat on a trailer is the freedom to go to different ports and overseas.

Rules and regulations change frequently, so contact the tourist and motoring authorities for the countries you intend trailing. While each country's regulations vary slightly, there are some common requirements that you must adhere to, irrespective of the country you are travelling to.

CHECKLIST FOR BOJANGLES BEFORE TOWING — Checked

Tie down straps
Wheel nuts tight
Bearings greased, tub of spare grease
Safety chains/lines (trailer to vehicle/boat to trailer)
Bag to cover prop
Spare wheel
Wing mirror extensions
Breakdown recovery membership card
Toolkit
Tailboard working
Jack & wheel nut spanner
Wheelclamp, keys & allen key
Tyres correctly inflated
Correct number plate
Jockey wheel secured
Boat keys!!!
Ski gear
Personal gear
Engine locked in position
Rope to use for launching
First aid kit/fire extinguisher

The tow vehicle

- Original insurance documents and overseas car and trailer insurance documents.
- The original registration documents for the vehicle.
- A set of spare bulbs and a warning triangle.

The boat

- The original sale documents to show tax has been paid.
- Insurance documentation.
- Make sure the boat's insurance cover is extended both for trailing and its use and mooring at the intended destination.
- Flare transportation could cause problems, as some countries require a firearms certificate for certain types of flare.

The crew

- A VHF certificate is recommended and is mandatory in some countries.
- Visas, if relevant.
- Most countries require an International Certificate of Competence (ICC) and some require a higher qualification. On inland waterways in Europe the CEVNI qualification will be required.
- Contact the country's national boating authority for details of compulsory certification required.

Buying and Owning a Boat

For most people, buying a boat is a considerable investment. However, in contrast to buying a house or car, the process can be very simple but you need to be aware of some of the pitfalls, especially when confirming ownership.

- Do your research - use website forums to learn of other people's views and experiences. Build up background knowledge of the type of boat you want to buy.

- Make sure the boat is suitable for its intended use. Planning and forethought will prevent you investing in a boat that you quickly 'outgrow'.

- Check magazines for a boat test on the boat you are interested in, many sell back issues of boat tests.

- Always seek proof of ownership via original invoices. As with a car a good service history and receipts indicate a good ownership trail.

- If buying from a dealer, is it a brokerage boat or one of their own craft? If it is their own boat you will have protection under the Sale of Goods Act.

- Establish that no finance company has a charge or ownership right over the vessel.

- Invest in a hull and engine survey – damaged and worn engines can be extremely expensive to fix.

- A 'low mileage' boat is not always the best. A boat that has been well looked after and run regularly can be a very good buy.

Insurance

Once you have bought your boat, insure it. Most marinas and harbours stipulate that you must be insured to keep your boat there.

Storage

Smaller boats are often stored on trailers, therefore trailing from home becomes an option. Many boatyards offer 'store and slip' facilities. Increasingly popular is storing your craft on a rack system where a forklift retrieves your boat then launches it when required. Keeping a boat out of the water removes the need for antifouling and allows it to dry out when not in use.

Larger boats are usually kept afloat in marinas or on moorings, although even boats up to 10m can be kept on racking systems.

Storage costs vary enormously. Popular marinas and storage sites are far more expensive than boatyards in less congested boating areas. Drying berths, buoys and pile moorings are all slightly cheaper than a marina but at the cost of convenience.

Boat care

Boat care is largely a matter of common sense:

- Wash the boat after each outing to remove salt deposits.
- If possible, flush water through the engine water intakes to avoid salt crystallisation in the cooling pipes.
- Keep batteries charged through the winter (remove them if they are not being used).
- Grease battery terminals with petroleum jelly to ensure the electrical connections remain good.
- Spray the electrics with a water repellent spray to keep water out.
- Consider spraying other exposed parts with a silicone spray.

Service intervals for engines vary according to the manufacturers' recommendations. High-usage boats may need to be serviced more than once a year, whereas boats used less frequently benefit from an end of season service and winterisation if they are not to be used during the winter.

SOLAS V

SOLAS V stands for 'Safety of Life at Sea Chapter V' and was created as a direct result of the Titanic disaster. In relation to smaller craft it places a number of requirements of Skippers, the main requirements are detailed below.

- **Radar Reflector** - Regulation 19.2.1.7.

All ships shall have, if less than 150 gross registered tonnes and if practicable, a radar reflector or other means, to enable detection by ships navigating by radar at both 9 and 3 GHz.

'When practicable' means that if you can carry a radar reflector, you should. Both passive radar reflectors and active devices are available.

- **Life-saving Signals** - Regulation 29.

An illustrated table describing the life-saving signals shall be readily available to the officer of the watch on every ship to which this chapter applies. The signals shall be used by ships or persons in distress when communicating with life-saving stations, maritime rescue units and aircraft engaged in SAR ops.

Keeping this table on board will mean that you comply with this regulation - the table can be found on pages 128/129.

- **Danger messages** - Regulation 31.

Masters are to communicate information on navigational dangers. These include, for example, a dangerous derelict or other dangerous obstructions, tropical storms, winds of Force 10 or more for which no warning has been received. The form that information is sent is not obligatory and it can be transmitted in plain language or using the International Code of Signals. Contracting governments must promulgate any danger information received and messages must be free of charge to ships.

This regulation basically means that you, as Skipper, have a responsibility to pass on information about navigation dangers to the Coastguard by any means that you can.

- **Danger messages -** Regulation 32.

This regulation deals with the kind of information required in danger messages. It also has examples of typical danger messages.

This regulation means that you should pass on sufficient information about any navigation dangers you experience or witness (For example: position, nature of danger, time seen/witnessed, any other useful information) to enable other shipping in the area to avoid it.

- **Distress messages -** obligations and procedures - Regulation 33.

Masters are obliged to respond to distress messages from any source. Ships can be requisitioned by the master of a ship in distress or the Search and Rescue (SAR) authorities.

This regulation reinforces the duty of skippers to respond to any distress messages they hear.

Safe navigation and avoidance of dangerous situations - Regulation 34.

Voyage planning is required on all vessels that go to sea. "Going to sea is defined as proceeding outside of categorized waters". You can get more information about what constitutes categorised waters from the MCA and the RYA.
MCA guidance notes say for 'small craft and pleasure vessels, the degree of voyage planning will be dependent on the size of vessel, its crew and the length of the voyage'. The MCA says that it 'expects all mariners to make a careful assessment of any proposed voyage taking into account all dangers to navigation, weather forecasts, tidal predictions and other relevant factors including the competence of the crew'.

Skippers should note that this regulation changes the status of passage planning on small boats from simply good practice to a requirement under UK law. No formal written plan is required and there is no set format.

Misuse of distress signals - Regulation 35.

"Distress signals only to be used for the proper purpose".

This regulation reinforces the fact that distress signals have a life saving role and should not be misused.

Bilges, it is illegal to pump out bilge water contaminated with oil. Use specialist kit to soak it up and dispose of in approved containers at marinas. Ensure fire extinguishers are not old illegal Halon versions.

At the helm, small sportsboats can get to places that larger craft can't. Take care not to disturb wildlife and vegetation in sensitive areas and consider the damage a prop can do in shallow water.

Heads, if you have a holding tank preferably use a pumping out station or pump out at least 3 miles offshore. Without a holding tank then try not to use the heads.

Galley, recycle waste wherever possible.

Anchoring & mooring, ensure you anchor where you won't damage the bottom and moor away from bankside habitats where you may disturb wildlife.

Antifoul, if applying antifoul then choose a product with the lowest levels of copper and biocide for your boat. Be careful to avoid spills.

Wash, choose an appropriate speed so as to not disturb other boaters, bankside wildlife and damage shore areas with your wash.

Refuelling, use a funnel to reduce the chances of spillage and have a spill kit to hand. Take care to mop up any spillages on deck.

Hull, when washing the hull or topsides choose environmentally friendly detergents.

Waste, secure rubbish and other loose items to avoid them being blown overboard. Discarded cigarette butts are often eaten by fish and gulls. Discard them responsibly.

Engine, use a 4 stroke outboard rather than a 2 stroke to increase fuel efficiency and reduce emissions.

Trailer, wash down your trailer carefully after each launch to reduce the chances of moving species from one area to another.

Life Saving Signals

To be used by Ships, Aircraft or Persons in Distress.

Maritime and Coastguard Agency

Search and Rescue Unit Replies
You have been seen, assistance will be given as soon as possible.

OR

Orange smoke flare.

Three white star signals or three light and sound rockets fired at approximately 1 minute intervals.

Surface to Air Signals

Note: Use International Code of Signal by means of lights or flags or by laying out the symbol on the deck or ground with items which have a high contrast to the background.

Message	International Code of Signals		ICAO Visual Signals
I require assistance	V ✕	●●●▬	V
I require medical assistance	W ▣	▬▬▬	X
No or negative	N ▦	▬●	N
Yes or affirmative	C ≡	▬●▬▬●	Y
Proceeding in this direction			↑

Air to Surface Direction Signals

Sequence of 3 manoeuvres meaning proceed to this direction.

1

Circle vessel at least once.

2

Cross low, ahead a vessel rocking wings.

3

Overfly vessel and head in required direction.

Your assistance is no longer required.

Cross low, astern of vessel rocking wings.

Note: As a non preferred alternative to rocking wings, varying engine tone or volume may be used.

Shore to Ship Signals

Safe to land here.

OR

K

Vertical waving of both arms, white flag, light or flare.　　Morse code signal by light or sound.

Landing here is dangerous. Additional signals mean safer landing in direction indicated.

OR

Horizontal waving of white flag, light or flare.
Putting one flag, light or flare on ground and moving off with a second indicates direction of safer landing.

S: ●●●
Morse code signals by light or sound.
R: ●━●
Land to the right of your current heading.
L: ●━●●
Land to the left of your current heading.

Air to Surface Replies

Message Understood.

OR　　　　　OR　　　　　OR

Drop a message.　Rocking wings.　Flashing landing or navigation lights on and off twice.　Morse code signal by light.

T 　 OR 　 R

Message Not Understood – Repeat.

OR　　　　　OR

Straight and level flight.　Circling.　Morse code signal by light.

R 　 P 　 T

Surface to Air Replies

Message Understood – I will comply.

OR　　　　　OR

Change course to required direction.

T
Morse code signal by light.

Code & answering pendant "Close Up".

I am unable to comply.

OR

N
Morse code signal by light.

International flag "N".

Glossary

Abeam – directly to either the left (port) or right (starboard) of the centre of a boat...... "the pier is directly abeam to port of us".

Aft – Towards the rear of a craft

A.P.E. – Assess, Plan, Execute – The thought process to go through prior to undertaking any boating manoeuvre.

Beam sea – The term used when a boat is travelling at 90° to the wind with waves approaching from one side of the boat.

Bearing – The angle from one object to another....."the rock bears 078°M from us"

Beaufort scale – A scale of wind strength

Bow – The front of the boat

Buoyancy aid – A type of Personal Floatation Device ('PFD') that is used for sports like waterskiing, windsurfing etc

Cardinal Marks – A type of buoyage used to mark an area of interest

Cathedral Hull – A type of hull typically found on craft like dories

Chine – The intersection between the vertical side of a boat's hull and the angled hull beneath.

Cleat – A T-shaped fitting used to attach mooring lines to. Found both on craft and pontoons.

Cone – The term applied to a shape used by sailing yachts. Also used to refer to a starboard lateral mark.

Course – The direction in which a craft is travelling over the ground. This could be different from the direction in which it is heading.

D-ring – An attachment point found on craft up to about 12m at the bow for towing or attaching a trailer winch strap.

Deep-V – A type of planing hull.

Deviation – The error induced in compass due to the effect of magnetic and electrical fields.

Displacement hull – A type of hull found on slower craft.

Dry suit – A suit worn for either watersports or in rougher weather that keeps the wearer fully dry.

DSC – Digital Selective Calling, the system used by newer VHF radios to send digital messages including distress.

Fairlead – A fitting in the bow area through which lines can be fed.

Following sea – The term applied when a craft is heading with the wind with the waves following the craft.

Freeboard – The height between the water level and the lowest part of the craft. In the case of a RIB this could be between the water level and the top of the tubes or the transom.

Give way vessel – The vessel that is required by the IRPCS to initially take action to avoid a collision.

GPS – Global Positioning System. A US led system used to define position and used in boat and vehicle satellite navigation systems.

Head sea – When a craft is heading directly into the waves/wind.

Heading – The direction in which a craft is pointing.

IALA – International Association of Lighthouse Authorities

IRPCS – International Regulations for Preventing Collisions at Sea – the 'Col Regs'

Jet drive – A type of drive system using a water jet for propulsion.

Kill cord – A critical item of safety equipment that when attached correctly to the person driving a boat kills the engine if they move away from the helm position.

Lateral marks – A type of buoyage system used to mark channels.

Leeward – The side of a boat furthest from the wind

Lifejacket – A type of Personal Floatation Device ('PFD')

Lifting strake – Also known as Running Strakes these are features on the hull of a planing boat that create lift and contribute to stability.

Making way – A vessel that is underway and is propelling itself through the water is making way.

Mayday – Where there is grave and imminent danger to a vehicle, vessel, aircraft or person and immediate assistance is required.

MMSI – Maritime Mobile Service Identify. The unique code programmed into a DSC radio to identify it.

MOB – Man overboard.

Neaps – A type of tide where the gravitational effect of the sun and moon is at its weakest giving rise to less pronounced high and low tides.

Outdrive – A type of drive system found with inboard engines. In effect is the lower half of an outboard and is moved by the steering to direct thrust.

Painter – The mooring line found on craft up to about 6m generally attached to the D-Ring.

Pan-Pan – A VHF call made to request assistance where life is not immediately at risk.

PFD – Personal Floatation Device.

Pivot point – The point about which a craft rotates when the steering is turned and thrust applied – can vary between forward and reverse.

Planing hull – The type of hull found on most fast powerboats

Plotter – A chartplotter, a system combining a GPS receiver and electronic charts that can show a craft's position and can be used for navigation.

Port – When facing forward in a boat the term applied to the left hand side of the craft.

Prop walk – Also known as 'paddle wheel effect'. An effect typically found on shaft driven boats where at the moment the throttle is engaged there is some sideways force before a forward force comes into effect.

Quarter – Found at the rear of the craft on either side of the craft.

RIB – A type of craft, 'Rigid Hull Inflatable Boat'. Also known as RHIB.

Route – A series of waypoints is joined together to form a route.

Scope – When referring to anchoring the length of line and chain that has been deployed.

Semi displacement hull – A type of hull

Shaft drive – A type of drive system where the engine drives the propeller via a metal shaft.

SOLAS V – 'Safety of Life at Sea Chapter V'.

Sponsons – Another name for the tubes on a RIB.

Spring – A line deployed when mooring to arrest forward or aft movement. Can be used to assist leaving a berth in more difficult conditions.

Springs – A tide where the combined gravitational effect of the sun and moon is at its greatest leading to the highest high tides and the lowest low tides.

Stand on vessel – In a potential collision situation the vessel that initially is required to hold its course and speed.

Starboard – When facing forward on a craft the right hand side of the vessel.

'Steer then gear' – The term Skippers use to remind themselves to ensure steering is pointing in the required direction before throttle is engaged.

Stern – The rear end of a craft

Stern drive – Also known as an 'Outdrive' a type of drive system akin to the lower half of an outboard that is attached to an inboard engine through the transom of a craft.

Stream – The term used to refer to the movement of tide or current.

Transom – The vertical surface at the rear of a craft that an outboard is attached to or through which the stern drives attach to the engine.

Underway – When a vessel ceases to be tethered to a pontoon or the seabed through its anchor it is underway.

Variation – The difference between the position of magnetic and true north.

VHF – A marine radio used for contacting other craft/stations and if necessary seeking assistance

Warp – Another name for a rope

Wash – The waves created by a boat's movement through the water.

Waypoint – When using a GPS unit or a chartplotter a point input into the unit to navigate to.

Wetsuit – Worn for watersports such as waterskiing. Allows a layer of water between the wearer and the suit to create warmth.

Windage – The effect of wind on a craft

Windward – The side of a boat nearest the wind

Index

Notes

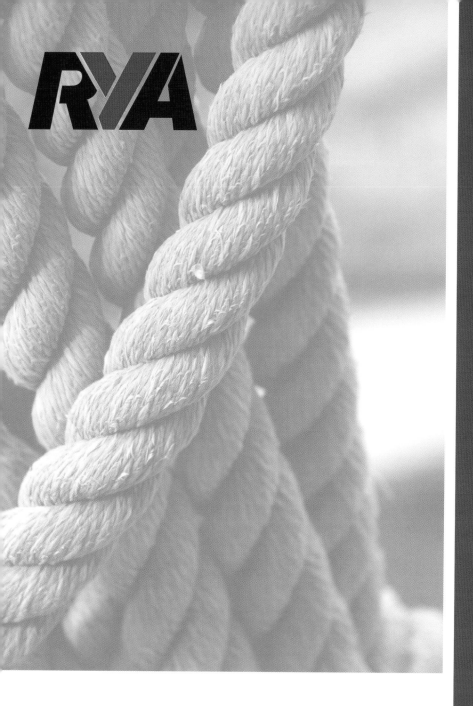

RYA

MEMBERSHIP

Promoting and Protecting Boating

www.rya.org.uk

**JOIN NOW
online at**
www.rya.org.uk